The SELAH *Journey*

A SACRED PATHWAY TO RECLAIMING YOUR PEACE, POWER, AND FREEDOM

The SELΛH *Journey*

A SACRED PATHWAY TO RECLAIMING YOUR PEACE, POWER, AND FREEDOM

CAMI RENÉE FOERSTER

The Selah Journey: A Sacred Pathway to
Reclaiming Your Peace, Power, and Freedom

Whistling Fox Publishing | Monument, Colorado

Edited by Domanie Spencer
Cover & Interior Design: George Stevens, G Sharp Design, LLC

ISBN: 979-8-9925946-0-7 (paperback)
ISBN: 979-8-9925946-1-4 (e-book)
Library of Congress Control Number: 2025905040

Disclaimer: This publication is designed to provide accurate and authoritative information regarding the subject matter covered. It is sold with the understanding that neither the author nor the publisher is engaged in rendering legal, investment, or accounting services. While the publisher and author have used their best efforts in preparing this book, they make no representations or warranties with respect to the accuracy or completeness of the contents of this book and specifically disclaim any implied warranties of merchantability or fitness for a particular purpose. The advice and strategies contained herein may not be suitable for your situation. You should consult with a professional when appropriate. Neither the publisher nor the author shall be liable for any loss of profit or any other commercial damages, including but not limited to special, incidental, consequential, personal, or other damages.

For all the helpers and caregivers, who give from their heart and soul, but sometimes forget that it is okay to receive help for yourself.

I see you. I am you. This book is for you.

TABLE OF CONTENTS

A NOTE OF CLARITY

This book is for all people: all cultures, all religions, all backgrounds, all beliefs, and all circumstances. With that in mind, I recognize that certain words can carry a feeling, tone, or nuance that may be uncomfortable for some. To diffuse some of that tension, allow me to explain my intended use of a few words you will find throughout this book.

In this book, I reference the ultimate source and power that gives rise to life on our planet. This origin and/or entity is referred to by many names and designations throughout our world. Whether you recognize this source from a scientific lens or a religious lens is entirely up to you. Throughout this book, I use the words Spirit and Creator to indicate this supreme life force for both the physical world and the spiritual world. It is my intention that with these more generic titles, capitalized to emphasize their ultimate status and place of honor in our lives, you can more easily adapt them to your own experiences and beliefs.

Also, when referring to Spirit and Creator with pronouns, I will use the S/He designation. I do this to respect all belief systems in general.

As this book is intended to be inclusive for all, when I speak to you—my reader—I do not know if you are male or female. Therefore, when I address or reference you with pronouns, I will alternate between she/her and he/him. I reserve they/them for plural or collective reference and use.

THE GOOD STUFF
BEFORE CHAPTER ONE

Hello, you!

Thank you for inviting me into your world. I know what a privilege it is to find a true and meaningful connection in this world, and I trust you will find a bit of that here in this book.

I wrote this book with you in mind. That might sound strange as it is likely we have never met. However, I share my story and insight here with the intention that it has found its way into the hands of those who are searching for both the inspiration and hope it contains. You see, I spent weeks in coffee shops, airports, hotel rooms, and in my own home office, imagining I was sitting across from you as I wrote. When I felt your presence, I allowed our conversation to pour through my fingers onto these pages. You now hold that very conversation in your hands.

You will undoubtedly get to know me better as you travel through these chapters, but allow me to give you a sneak peak of who I am at the start of our dialogue.

As the firstborn kid in my family, I was always the little helper. As I grew up, it became clear that being a helper went beyond being a role I filled within my family; it was actually a core part of my personality. One of the first times I realized this (but didn't fully appreciate it yet) was when my peers voted me "Most Helpful" during my final year of high school. Over three decades later, a personality assessment known as the Enneagram continued to affirm this truth by revealing me as Type 2: The Helper. All my life I have been a helper. It is hardwired into my personality in such a way that I instinctually want to help others, to a fault at times!

One of my motivations for writing this book is that I want to be a helper to you. I believe my experiences, my emotions, my struggles and successes, my fears and hopes, are not unique to me. They are common throughout humanity. While our circumstances may be different, we have in common our attempts to find meaning and purpose as we live our lives. If my stories and experiences can be of service to others, especially to you, then I want to share them so we can learn from one another.

I am also a wanderlust. I seek out and experience a special freedom in road-tripping across America and exploring the world. Life is a journey! Travel language and imagery are prevalent throughout my writing. So, during our time together, you will undoubtedly notice all kinds of traveling language as we move through the content. Even the title, The Selah Journey, reflects this reality for me. It is both a specific trip we can plan for ourselves to help us intentionally build our rhythms and awareness of self-care, as well as a framework for our life, providing foundational practices to implement as we build freedom and alignment with our truest self. Whether your Selah Journey begins in the comfort of your own home, or during a trip to explore our incredible world, I'm glad to be along for the ride.

Another glimpse of "Cami in a nutshell" is that in every season of my life, I have been mentoring, teaching, guiding, training, and coaching others in their self-improvement. From teaching the letters of the alphabet to kindergarteners when I was eleven to creating personal development plans for my resident advisor staff in college, I have found great joy in helping (there is that word again!) others recognize their potential and find ways to expand into that potential. It is no surprise I have found my ideal career in life coaching!

One other foundational part of who I am is my spirituality. I have connected with Spirit throughout my whole life. This part of my journey has taken me through many different expressions of Christianity and has allowed me to develop a deep appreciation for the role of spirituality and faith in the lives of my friends around the world. Sharing my experiences of faith will reveal some of my Christian beliefs and values. Although my faith journey has had its ups and downs, it is an integral part of who I am. If you have a faith practice, I hope it is also a foundational part of who you are. No matter how our spirituality is expressed in our lives, The Selah Journey has so much to offer all of us.

These qualities (and a few more) are what have led me to share The Selah Journey with you. It needs to be more than a best-kept secret. This is a pathway that has led me to a place of more contentment, more understanding, and more freedom. If it can lead you into these same places I will be overjoyed! Let's shout this from the rooftops!

So, take this book as a conversation between friends. I'll share some of my stories, and hopefully, you will be stirred to remember some of yours. Finding common ground in our experiences, you can ask questions in the margins and record your reactions and thoughts within the text as you read. Take a peek into the Nerd Nook with me and explore some of our conversations in greater detail. Take in the contents with a spot of tea, a cup of coffee, or a glass of wine. Or even a dram of whiskey, on occasion.

When you reach the end of the book, I hope you feel empowered to begin your personal Selah Journey into a more fulfilling life. If you desire to continue the conversation, scan the QR code in the back to see what we are exploring in our Selah Journey community. Or visit our website at www.theselahjourney.com to discover which next steps feel right for you.

It is my pleasure to share this time with you. I trust it can guide you, encourage you, and inspire you wherever life finds you right now.

In Gratitude,

Cami

The
PATHWAY

CHAPTER 1

SELAH—YOUR MAP

apologize. You might not be familiar with the word *Selah* yet. Perhaps you have a niggling sense in your head that you have heard that word before but cannot quite place it. It is not exactly a common word. In fact, it is an ancient word. I remember when I first became aware of that word: Selah. It is a memory impressed upon my heart.

As a college student living in New England in the early 1990s, my friends and I would take full advantage of pleasant days. You know those days, when it is warm enough and dry enough to spread a blanket on the grass and soak up the rays of sunshine along with the warmth of friends and daydreams. In this particular memory, I was with my dear friend, Emily, and we were imagining some of the possible futures the coming years might hold. We watched a dragonfly dance around our blanket and spoke of the men we hoped to date and the lives we hoped to build. We also imagined creating a place, like a retreat center, where *Selah* was celebrated and people could come to enjoy a space to receive rest and rejuvenation.

Selah. It was a word we had recently become enamored with in our biblical studies classes. A word hiding in plain sight. You see, *Selah* is found primarily in the poetry of the Psalms in the Hebrew Bible (also known as the Old Testament in Christianity). It is not found in the middle of the verses of poetry. Rather, when you look at the structure of the verses on the page, it is hanging out on the right-hand margin, often in italics. *Selah.*

This clever word gives direction to the reader. It is a request for the reader to take a moment to pause their reading, consider what they just took in, and respond with thanks or praise for what they just received. It asks the reader to rest, reflect, and practice gratitude in the midst of their experience of the poem.

My friend and I were wondering what it could look like for Selah to be enacted in our lives. What might it look like to build a space where people could take to heart the actions of resting, reflecting, and expressing gratitude as self-care practices? It is not hard to imagine why we might play with that idea. College was full of activity, work, and personal growth. There always seemed to be too much to do and not enough time to do it all. We prided ourselves on our accomplishments, most of which were earned through sleep deprivation. The concept of self-care seemed amazing, but out of reach. Wouldn't it be nice if a place existed where we could go and catch up on the rest and restoration that our schedules prohibited? So that afternoon, we played with the idea of selah within our imaginations.

Little did I know that thirty years later I would still be in love with that odd little word—selah—and exploring what it could mean for myself and others. For you.

Full disclosure: during those thirty-plus years since college, I amassed a terrible track record when it came to self-care. My personality type is wired to people please and to be helpful to others above all else. My faith background values sacrificial service to others. My ego likes to be liked. In my world, these three drives combined to make me a walking self-care disaster. I wonder if you can relate (wink, wink)? Life had a way of convincing me that my existence found more meaning when I gave my best, taking good care of my family, my religion, my neighborhood, my job, my community, my friends, and my dog. Only after all of this, whatever time and resources were left, which was usually not much, could be used to care for myself. During these years, my head understood that this lifestyle wasn't completely sound. However, my desire to be needed, loved, respected, useful, and worthy inwardly persuaded and overruled the logical fact that it was okay for me to be cared for too.

This life of putting everyone else first has a way of sneaking up on us. Maybe we are a bit tired, but at least the to-do list got done. Maybe we feel sad or weepy, but we don't know why. Maybe we become indecisive because others in our lives have strong opinions, and we can't find the energy to have our own opinions. Perhaps our anxiety gets triggered because we can't seem to do enough, or we don't know what needs to be done next. Hopelessness might appear when we can see we are stuck but cannot find a pathway towards change. We might wonder if we would have any value to others if we stopped doing all the things and just took a moment to be.

Or maybe all those "maybes" and "mights" are just me. But maybe they seem familiar to you too.

Eventually, living a life where I came last on my list became my undoing. My body finally screamed for my attention in the form of a panic attack while I was solo driving through the Colorado mountains. Shaking and sobbing, I was physically halted in my tracks and had to face the fact that something was terribly wrong. After the wave of panic washed over me, I carefully completed my ride home. Every fiber in my body wanted to run away. Driving home, I realized home had become my place of stress instead of safety. If I expected anything to change, I needed to do things differently. I followed my instincts (along with guidance from Spirit), quickly packed up some camping gear, and drove 1200 miles (approximately 2000 kilometers) away from home to find space to listen to what my body was telling me. My undoing became the very first step of my Selah Journey, the pathway back to me.

NERD NOOK:
LONG-TERM EFFECTS OF STRESS

A handful of years prior to the COVID-19 global pandemic, the World Health Organization (WHO) labeled stress as the "Health Epidemic of the 21st Century." Information about stress abounds as a quick internet search will confirm. Stress is a common experience that humans encounter on a daily basis. In simple terms, stress is the force or tension we experience that demands a response. It signals to us that something is out of balance, disrupting our equilibrium. Seen in this light, stress itself is neutral, neither good nor bad. It is how we interpret stress that shades our experience in positive or negative tones.

Simplified, the natural pattern of a stress response is as follows: the brain perceives a threat, and your hormonal systems release adrenaline and cortisol to stimulate your body to respond to the threat. Once the perceived threat is resolved, your body systems return to normal functioning. However, experiencing chronic, prolonged stress or repeated periods of stress allows the stress response to continue unchecked. As a result, physical, emotional, and behavioral issues become present which interfere with a person's typical daily functioning.

When we carry long-term stress, we increase our risk for many health issues. A quick survey of the WHO and the Mayo Clinic websites reveals that prolonged stress can lead to:

- Anxiety and depression
- Digestive problems
- Headaches
- Muscle tension and pain
- Heart disease and heart attacks
- High blood pressure
- Strokes
- Sleep problems and disturbances

- Weight gain
- Memory and concentration problems
- Increased alcohol and tobacco use

The bottom line is that when it is left unchecked, chronic stress will hasten your death. That may sound harsh, but it is absolutely true. In this case, ignorance is not bliss. Many reputable mental health websites have resources for you to evaluate your stress level and provide tips to help you start better managing the stress you are experiencing. If you live with chronic stress, please partner with a health care provider or another wellness provider and begin addressing the health issues that stress has imposed upon you. In my life, I put off the warning signs of stress until a panic attack stopped me in my tracks. Please learn from my neglect. Although we cannot avoid all the stress we encounter throughout life, it doesn't mean we have to let it rob us of living our lives in full and rewarding ways.

My Selah Journey Begins

That drive began a hiatus from my life that placed me on a journey back to myself. How could I afford to take time away from the responsibilities and obligations in my life? I couldn't. However, I had become so thoroughly and completely lost and overwhelmed during the previous years that I had reached my breaking point. I could not continue in a life that had slowly allowed me to disappear within my own home.

I didn't know this trip was going to become my Selah Journey at first. I fled my Colorado life so quickly that I didn't have time to come up with a plan. I just headed toward the one place that called to me—my childhood home in Northern California. As I pulled onto the property that used to be home, I was confronted with the evidence of the fire that had decimated our community just a few short years before. Cracked concrete foundations and dug-out depressions were all that land held to remind me of the spaces I had grown up in. Only a handful of what used to be hundreds of tall pine and cedar trees on the land remained, their sheltering presence erased leaving a scattering of wide stumps in the ground. Looking back, I'm sure the land called me to return to her. We were both lost, wild, and recovering from devastation. We both had to find a new way of being in this world.

There is an image of a tree I captured during the beginning of my Selah Journey. It is the remnants of an oak tree that used to tower over my dad's garage in the backyard. Now it is a ghostly hollowed-out trunk just a few feet taller than me. The interior is black where the core of the tree used to be. I posted it to my social media on July 23, 2021, with these words:

I can't stop looking at this tree. It is next to my campsite and my eyes are continually drawn to it. It is hauntingly beautiful—only a shadow of its living glory. It is a signpost of a past tragedy that it could not recover from.

Some of you have asked me, what is The Selah Journey? I will tell more in the coming days, but for now, The Selah Journey is a way for me to heed the warning of this tree.

Difficult and tragic things happen in life and the way we carry them makes an impact on our whole being. I do not want to be destroyed by the trials and disasters that I encounter. Rather, while they may shape me a bit, I want to nurture a strong, grounded, healthy core so that tragedy can pass over me, but not gut me like this tree.

The Selah Journey is how I grow into that ability to withstand loss and challenge. My journey is pointing out a lot of neglected and dead things I have been carrying within me and these places are pleading with me for some restoration. So, I am resting A LOT to restore my weary soul; I am entering spaces to ponder and reflect on things my head and heart are grasping at; I am seeking to recognize moments that are beautiful, good, and praiseworthy to foster gratitude and joy in my life.

My Selah Journey is unfolding one day at a time. I am thankful for each of you who have chosen to join me. #theselahjourney

Only three short years after my post with that tree, my life began to testify to a journey of continuing personal transformation and growth that was inconceivable when I took the picture in that post. In the three years of continued Selah Journeying, I have:

- Learned how to prioritize rest for my body, soul, and spirit, allowing healing from past stress and trauma to take root.
- Let go of self-loathing and embrace the reality that my unique and perfectly imperfect self has much to offer the world as long as I live.
- Explored new hobbies and activities like crocheting and scuba diving to learn more about what I like and what brings me enjoyment.
- Taken opportunities to explore the world and learn from the different people and cultures we share a globe with.
- Embraced my intuitive nature and experienced a wholeness and freedom I haven't felt since my childhood.
- Become a published author and developed the courage I needed to find my voice and share my story.
- Grown to like, even love, who I am and who I am continuing to become, with gratitude and awe.

These milestones, and many more, were made possible because of The Selah Journey and the five core pillars it introduced into my life. Moving from a place of despair and hopelessness into a way of joy and empowerment felt unattainable, yet the proof is in the transformation. The core pillars of The Selah Journey have become my trail markers along the journey. I look for them, learn from them, and go out of my way to incorporate them into my trip. At this moment, I have been given just this one life. Leaning into these signposts helps me to make the most out of what I have been given.

The Five Pillars of The Selah Journey

Let's take a quick peek at the framework of The Selah Journey. Think of this as an overview of a map to make sure we do not miss any of the main stops along our way.

I Choose Me

The very first thing we do, and need to persist in every single day, is allowing ourselves to be important. This is your journey. You are in the driver's seat so it is entirely important that you choose to be a priority. Choose to allow yourself to be worthy of the care and consideration you need. Choose to show yourself love, grace, and gratitude. Choose to acknowledge that you, the right-here-and-now you, are not only worthy of love and kindness but deserve to be cared for, and cared for especially by your own precious self.

This may sound challenging, and that is okay. It also may sound a bit counter to prevailing wisdom. When I first received the words "I Choose Me" for The Selah Journey, I thought it sounded too self-centered. I worried it would justify or excuse selfishness and overinflated egos. Words are heard in nuanced ways, depending on the experiences and mindset of the one who hears the words. To be clear, this is what I Choose Me means, for us.

I Choose Me means I am just as important as the person next to me. Not more important, nor less important. I am **as**

*I am
just as
important
as the
person
next to me.*

important as someone else. It means that if I can listen and extend compassion and care towards a friend, or even a stranger in my life, then I can also receive the same care and compassion when it is extended to me. It means I can honestly embrace my strengths and feel proud of my accomplishments. It means I am worthy of respect as a fellow human being. It extends the golden rule of "Do unto others what you would have them do unto you" in both directions. The way I treat others is just as important as the way I treat myself.

Sabbath Resting

Our second journey marker along our path reveals a critical stop that is often skipped over or hurried through because it is never considered a destination: the rest stop. Along a road trip, when we feel tired or hungry or need to stretch our legs, the rest stop is a place to do just that. For The Selah Journey, Sabbath Resting is just the stop we need to explore.

Let me ask you a question. When did we forget that rest is just as important to us as food, water, security, and companionship? When did resting become a weakness in the landscape of activity and accomplishments? At what point did we allow the self-sacrifice of sleep to be an acceptable price for creating a good life? Once upon a time I believed these things and would ignore my need for sleep to prove to the world how hard-working I was. I would complain about how exhausted I felt while insisting that I had too much to do before I could allow myself to take a break. Weariness became my badge of honor.

I realize there are seasons in our lives when rest may be harder to come by. I remember when my children were babies, and they would fight sleep for the first years of their lives. As a mother, my body and heart were so attuned to them that when they awoke, so did I. I even remember baby-talking with my infant son in that sing-songy voice, telling him that he was the "cutest and most precious little torturer I knew." Night after night of sleep deprivation was the standard pattern. As never-ending as those seasons feel when we are in the midst of them, they are just that—a season. When we are in the midst of those seasons, actively finding ways to adjust is essential while we look for the opportunity to move into healthier rhythms as quickly as possible.

Sabbath Resting is learning to live in a rhythm that allows you intervals to practice resting as if your work was done. Did you catch that? *As if your work was done.* It means honoring the value of slowing down and decompressing from life's demands. It involves protecting space in your life for play, creativity, and restoration. It can feel like taking a deep breath and stepping away from the crazy stress and energy of the world for a minute so you can connect with what is truly important. You.

The Gift of Reflection

Continuing along our map, we notice the symbol for a roadside curiosity, those thought-provoking locations that stir up curiosity, wonder, and exploration. The Gift of Reflection is just such a stop, like seeing the largest rocking chair in the world or the geographical center of the United States. When we dedicate a bit of time to those spaces that pique our interest and prime our imagination, we can learn a bit about ourselves, the world we are exploring, and what we want to carry with us as we continue on.

The truth is, you are a wonder! Instead of rushing through life and snapping a photo for the digital scrapbook, what would happen if you chose to linger with questions and observations that arise for you along the way? Sometimes your surroundings can prompt a metaphor that describes your life experience, giving you a gift of insight. Sounds and scents can stir up memories that build connections between the past and present versions of yourself, allowing you a moment to be your own guide. The feel of the wind in your hair or the sun on your face can stir up a dormant emotion, revealing an undercurrent of feelings you may be avoiding out of fear or overwhelm.

Slowing down and paying attention to our whole selves, we discover the beauty of The Gift of Reflection. It allows space for us to ask questions and allow the responses to unfold in an unforced way. Boredom has a way of sparking creativity and perspective, so get a little bored! In doing so, we can discover insights, understanding, and connections that were waiting to be revealed in a time of reflection. Protecting this time and space will deliver gifts of truth and wisdom which we are all the better for receiving.

Gratitude and Praise

The scenic vista provides a beautiful moment along a road trip. It invites you to pull off highways and byways to absorb a bit of the world's beauty. This stop costs nothing but time and gives you inspiration and awe in return. I have experienced gorgeous mountain lakes mirroring the golden aspen trees along their banks in their smooth waters, and sheltered nooks within redwood trees that beckon you to believe in the faeries and magic that exists within the veils of sunbeams speckling the forest floor. The vistas vary along every journey, but the joy and beauty of these stops provide unforgettable moments throughout your trip.

Our scenic vistas along The Selah Journey are the practices of Gratitude and Praise. It costs us nothing to look for the good and beauty in the world. When we seek it, we find what we are looking for because it is all there just waiting for us to notice it and receive it. Gratitude is the kindness we give ourselves by letting the good penetrate our souls where it nourishes our hearts and heals past hurts. Praise is giving this same kindness to others by calling out the good in them and sharing our appreciation with them as a gift of joy. These vistas are free and priceless.

Your current circumstances may make this practice hard to embrace. Maybe it sounds too easy and too good to be true. I remember feeling that way myself before my Selah Journey began. Not only that, I even feared that in order to find something good, I may be fooling myself by making something up that didn't really exist. I didn't trust myself to recognize false hope, and I felt too wounded to risk more disappointment in myself. Please hear me; it is okay to be exactly where you are right now. And I promise you, the good is there. It is real and you will find it.

My Selah Tribe

Every road trip I have ever taken involves people. From complete strangers to lifelong friends, all types of people become part of my travels. Our Selah Journey map will take us to some of these places where our people are, and they enrich our journey! Sometimes we get to extend help and friendship to others, and sometimes we receive these gifts ourselves. People can provide

It costs us nothing to look for the good and beauty in the world.

connection, perspective, and warnings along the way. The point is, my trips are usually better for the people I encounter along the way.

As we travel along The Selah Journey, our community and tribe are indispensable. We are not meant to do life alone. Others provide insight and information for us in a timely way that we may not be able to access on our own. A perspective, a thought-provoking question, an encouragement, a truth, a validation, a helping hand, or a witness are all precious nuggets our tribe gives us. As we embark on our Selah Journey, it is wise to consider whom we trust to support us along the way.

While some in our tribe may take the journey with us, at least for part of the time, there will be others we encounter along the way. No matter who they are or how much time we spend with them, each person has a unique role to play as we travel along our path. Each one is a testament to the power and strength a community provides along our transformation. I have deep gratitude and love for all of those who held space for me in my first physical Selah Journey, and for those who continue to do so as I continue along this path of transformation. Your tribe will hold an important space in your story as you embark on your Selah Journey and become better acquainted with a truer and more aligned version of yourself.

The

PERSON

CHAPTER 2

YOU ARE HERE

I wish I could share an easier story with you. But I can see you there, seated across from me, waiting to hear if I will be honest and share my story in all of its raw emotions and life-changing force. You deserve to know why I hold out The Selah Journey as a lighthouse to be trusted in a sea of chaos.

How did I get here? How did I reach the point in my life where running away from my home, my family, my responsibilities...running away from my whole life...seemed like my only option? How in the world did I allow that to happen? The truth is, there isn't one satisfying answer. Like death by a thousand paper cuts, I had reached my point of desperation by making a million small decisions which eventually created a life that was killing me.

Looking back through the decade that led up to my desperate road trip reveals warning signs that I ignored or denied in the name of just doing what needed to be done.

Grief rolled through my life in perpetual waves. Within a span of six years, loss after loss created layers of grief. I lost my dream job out of the blue in a wave of restructuring. I lost my community of twenty-plus years to a move. I lost my hometown, my anchor, to a wildfire. I lost my dad to a stroke. I lost my sense of self to depression. These losses all happened in the midst of life—raising my kids and rebuilding our family rhythms in a new community. The grief of compounded loss would come in waves and felt inconvenient. I didn't have time for it! So, I would push it away to be dealt with on another day. The problem was, I never allowed that other day to arrive.

Health struggles persisted. I have a long history of major depressive disorder. My longest season in this particular valley of depression lasted over eight years. During this time, the practices I had typically relied on in the past to manage the load fell short. Not only that, but I was unaware of the impact long-term stress was having on my body. Weight gain, systemic inflammation, stress, and anxiety attacks became my norm. Not even an overnight stay in the hospital was enough to wake me up from my denial.

Fear pushed me deeper into people-pleasing. These years of struggle made me feel vulnerable. In order to make me feel better, I turned towards continual acts of service. I wanted to please others so that they wouldn't see how messed up I truly felt. Sacrificial service became my norm, and I threw out any remaining healthy boundaries. I would not say "no" to others because I needed to be needed. I feared feeling useless. I wrestled

"*What looks like our undoing becomes our gateway into becoming.*"

with imposter syndrome and viewed myself as a fraud always on the verge of being exposed. I denied who I authentically was in order to be who I thought others wanted or needed me to be.

Continually ignoring the warning signs, I kept telling myself that others were more important than myself. I didn't realize my self-neglect was keeping me stuck and my home was becoming a prison of my own making. Eventually, the all-encompassing pain I experienced broke me. Change could no longer wait.

How Did I Get Here?

Every Selah Journey starts right where we are at the very moment we decide that something needs to change. That is our starting point. While our stories are surely different, sometimes when we hear someone else's experience, we see a bit of ourselves in their story and we sense a connection. It is one of the reasons we love to read books and watch movies. Whether the people are fictional or historical, we can see a part of ourselves in their struggles. We can identify with, be inspired by, and learn from one another as we put ourselves in someone else's shoes.

How about you? Have you ever asked yourself, "How did I get here?" Have you stopped and wondered, "What did I do that led me to this space?" Is it not where you intended to be, nor where you hoped you would land at this point in your life? Maybe things look okay on the outside for someone glancing in your direction, but inside, you know the full and beautiful life you dream of feels like an illusion or a mirage. A life that remains just out of reach.

Embarking on a new journey requires you to know where you are starting from. Even if you feel lost, taking a moment to note the details of your starting point can help you along the way. Take note of your current circumstances and surroundings. Some things you cannot change or influence, but to ignore them would be foolish. Take note of your thoughts. What are the stories you continue to tell yourself? What thoughts or ideas play on repeat in your mind? Are your thought patterns focused and clear or scattered and foggy? Take note of your heart and emotions. Maybe you have shut down your feelings and have allowed a dull numbness to become your norm. Maybe your emotions are so overwhelming that you feel constantly on edge with fear or grief. Take note of your body. Are you weary of that beyond-tired exhaustion that makes everything seem harder? Do you get headaches regularly? Are you carrying so much tension in your body that something always hurts? Is your stomach in knots with anxiety, or have you lost your appetite altogether?

The truth is as human beings we avoid change. We will allow many things to persist in our lives in order to maintain some type of status quo. For me, it often looks like excuses and procrastination. I justify behaviors that I know are holding me back from the progress I say that I desire. I blame my circumstances for depriving me of the opportunity to make the necessary and desired changes in my life. I focus more on the ways I fail at taking action than I do celebrating the steps forward that I do take.

Until we are sick and tired of being sick and tired, we avoid change consciously and subconsciously. However, when it all becomes too much, when we hit our breaking point, when we lose our shit out of desperation for change—that is the golden moment. The moment when change becomes inevitable. What looks like our undoing becomes our gateway into becoming.

Embracing Transformation

Let's chat about change for a moment. More accurately, let us talk about transformation. As we set out from our starting point, The Selah Journey is not merely about a change that may or may not be permanent. There are many things we can change about ourselves—our attitudes, our habits, and our circumstances—but these are all things we can change back by returning to our former ways of life. What we are seeking with The Selah Journey is an inner transformation that is lasting—a metamorphosis of you.

A beautiful and precious example of this metamorphic transformation for me was the process by which I became a mother. When I was twenty-six years old, to my joy I discovered I was pregnant. For nine months I grew in every way as I became aware of this new precious life growing inside me. Hearing her heartbeat for the first time was magical. Feeling the flutters of her moments in my belly reminded me that my body held an entirely unique human. We played "tag" when she would stretch her foot out and I would gently push back. As she grew, I grew. Not only in size but my focus, my energy, and my heart grew to include her in every aspect of my life. And then came the labor! Things did not go smoothly, and the birthing pains were like nothing I had ever experienced or imagined before. However, the moment she was born and placed on top of my belly, my eyes witnessed her for the first time and I was transformed. Never again would I go back to my former life and never would I want to. When I birthed my daughter, she also birthed me into a completely new being. I was a mother, and that would never change as long as I lived.

What is beautiful about this metamorphosis is that it is uniquely mine. Many others have become parents. My husband's transition into fatherhood was different from my experience. My mother's experience was different from mine. My friends and other family members each have had unique pathways to the transformation into parenthood. My story includes my rhythms, my health, my cravings, my headaches, my labor, my preparation, my thoughts, my fears, and my joys. All of these pieces made my experience unique and let me into a transformed existence. My children are now a forever part of me.

In the same way, you are at the starting point of your own personal metamorphosis. A transformed way of being you in this world. The day you step onto the pathway of your Selah Journey, you are choosing to open yourself up in ways that will transform your heart, your mind, and your being. This is a journey towards a more aligned and integrated you. The pillars and tools of The Selah Journey will keep you on the path and moving towards the goal. You will likely experience a range of human emotions: from confusion to wonder, from sorrow to joy, from anger to acceptance. They may be fantastic revelations. There will probably be some painful memories to revisit. Like a caterpillar in its chrysalis, you may feel like you have been reduced to a pile of goo! There will be moments of enlightenment and new understandings. All of this will become your unique story of transformation. Unlike anyone else, you will begin to shine as the incredibly brilliant individual you are.

This incredible and significant transformation happens one step at a time. If you have tried to make life changes before, such as a New Year's Resolution to go to the gym more regularly, you probably started off by reworking your schedule, purchasing a gym membership, and attempting to accomplish your goal with

"Honesty with ourselves leads us to the truth."

one firm and challenging decision. The adjustment can feel great at the start, but then one little extra rest day sneaks into your week. And then your workload picks up and you miss another day. Or one morning you wake up really exhausted and decide you need sleep more than you need a workout and you hit the snooze button as you roll over in bed. When we attempt dramatic goals with big sweeping changes, we will eventually experience some form of self-sabotage. It happens to us all! But why?

Our bodies and minds love to hold the status quo. They find a point of equilibrium in our lifestyle and create a set point in our bodies to hold us at our "normal" state. They want to maintain normalcy. Big changes might be tolerated for a short time because we are adaptable and can rise to a new challenge. Willpower and determination are powerful tools to initiate a change. However, our mind and body will quickly desire to return to the "normal" state we started from. Before a new routine is established, we unconsciously begin to sabotage the very changes we set out to achieve. If this is the case, how can we move into the lasting changes we desire?

I call it the "trickle effect." Instead of trying to make big life changes, we start by making small shifts instead. Little adjustments to our "normal" way that do not set off alarm bells in our mind and body. To illustrate, when I first started drinking coffee, I needed to have it with sugar and cream to offset the bitterness. Eventually, the time came when I was looking to cut some unnecessary calories from my diet to meet new health goals. It felt too daunting to go from a luxurious vanilla latte to straight black coffee in one go. I knew I would tolerate it for a short time, and then go back to the established habit of choosing the sugared-up latte. Instead, I slowly began to decrease the amount of sugar, little by little, over the course of a few weeks. Once I eliminated the sugar, I repeated the gradual process with the cream until I was finally drinking black coffee and absolutely loving the flavors of it. Transitioning in small increments allowed my mind to accept the changes without feeling like something was drastically different. The alarm bells of change stayed quiet, and I didn't feel like I was missing out on anything during the process. Eventually, I became a proud, black coffee drinker. Using the small, gradual steps of the trickle effect helped me to avoid the self-sabotage trap.

NERD NOOK:
THE MIND-BODY CONNECTION

The mind and body are inextricably linked together in a dance of equilibrium. As physical beings, survival is our top, instinctual priority. To ensure our survival, our body takes in information through our physical senses, communicates to our magnificent brains, and the appropriate response is distributed to the rest of our bodily systems to equip us with what is needed. All of this happens without us even realizing it in our autonomic nervous system.

Simply speaking, this system functions within our nervous system. The polyvagal theory describes the function of vagus nerve which runs from our brain, through our spinal cord, and extends throughout the front and back of our bodies. It connects our brain, our heart, and our gut as it receives and sends information. This nerve is what signals to our body if we should be in: (1) a fight-or-flight response to flee or fight off danger, (2) a freeze response that immobilizes us for self-preservation in extreme danger, or (3) a calmly engaged response of safety and connection.

When this system works well, it adjusts through the day to keep us pointed to a centered and thriving place of safety and productivity. When stressors increase a bit, this vagus nerve steps on the gas to give us a bit more energy and focus to navigate through the perceived issue, then returns to being safely engaged in our space. When the stress is elevated to a survival level, the freeze response may put on the brakes to immobilize us, concentrating our energy reserves on our brain, heart, and lungs for self-preservation.

These systems are designed to work together to help us navigate all our daily encounters. Throughout a typical day, we might engage with the calm and safety of our home, the stress of work and traffic, the satisfaction of a good meal, and the tension of a strained relationship. Our systems regulate the ebb and flow of all this energy and stimulation to allow our body opportunities for both activity and rest. However, sometimes we are exposed to extreme and/or prolonged stressors that keep our vagus nerve system stuck in the "on" position. When this happens, our mind-body keeps a record of what those stressors are so that the next time we encounter them, instead of ramping up into an alerted state, it just floors the gas into full gear, overreacting and overcommitting to the perceived threat. This is what we commonly refer to as Post Traumatic Stress.

It is possible to reacclimate our system to a more appropriate response level through a gradual and worthwhile process. As we explore our past stories and experiences along The Selah Journey, be mindful that we may trigger an unexpected reaction. Because our mind-body connection is vigilant at protecting us, a memory, smell, or sensation may activate our fight-or-flight response or even a freeze response. While it may feel alarming when this happens, this is a fantastic learning opportunity. It provides us with essential information to unpack the experience and retrain our mind-body connection back into a place of balance and health. If this happens to you, please seek out the help of a trained psychiatrist to support you on your journey back to your best self.

Traveling Essentials

One thing I insist that you bring with you are two essential attitudes: *honesty* and *curiosity*. While this may seem obvious, my experience has taught me it is harder than it looks. You see, as we move through life, we translate our experiences and their connected emotions into stories. These are the stories we tell ourselves. For example, during my grade school years, I was encouraged to do my best in school. Turned out, I had an aptitude for scholastic learning so this came easily to me. Continuing to get high marks, I felt seen and loved when my parents recognized my achievements. However, since my personal average became high marks, I only remember being recognized for my perfect scores on my report card. My emotions of feeling loved became attached to the experience of perfect marks. As a result, the story I told myself became that I knew I was loved because I had perfect marks.

As we grow up, we understand ourselves as the center of our world. We see everything from our own perspective. Everything we experience feels personal. Our perspective revolves around how others respond to and affect us. Our story develops with us at the center. As we mature, our awareness expands and we learn that instead of being the center of our world, we are part of a community or a family in which many different perspectives coexist. We come to recognize that not everything is personally directed towards us. Our stories are a combination of what has occurred combined with our internal interpretation of how and why it happened that way.

Learning that the stories we tell ourselves can be separated into the actions we remember, and our interpretations of these actions gives us an incredible ability to reevaluate the stories, we can cast off some of the false beliefs that no longer serve us. Now that I have a few more years of experience, I know the conclusion

I came to as a young child of being loved when I was perfect was inaccurate. Through *honest* examination of the experiences I had, and the emotions attached to them, I can now see how the story I told myself of being loved when I was perfect was not true. It may have helped me push to excel as a child, but as an adult, it hinders me from trying new things because I'm afraid that failure and imperfection might mean I'm unlovable. Using honesty and curiosity, I can identify and separate my interpretation of the events from the actual experience and update my beliefs from a more mature perspective. For example, when my report card recorded an A/A+, I was rewarded with money. That meant I had achieved my best because I received a reward. That correlation was so strong for me that I did not allow myself to get anything less, for fear it would not be considered "my best." When I add the tool of curiosity to this experience, I can explore other interpretations. For example, did my parents scold me for less-than-perfect scores? Not that I remember. Did they ever withhold love when I fell short? No. What might have been their intention for the standard of "do your best?" Was it for me to achieve perfection? Not likely. Could it have been to encourage me to keep trying and put my best effort forward no matter the result? More likely.

Applying the twin tools of *honesty* and *curiosity* allows us to gain new perspectives and insights we didn't have when our stories were first created. So why do we resist applying honesty to our past stories? What hinders us from being honest with ourselves? Remember how our whole being tends to resist big changes? When we use the lens of honesty in looking into the stories that have led up to our current life, we are opening ourselves up to learning how much of what we remember is based upon fact, and what is based upon our interpretations. We shift the focus from blaming others for what has happened to us and begin to accept responsibility for how we understood and responded to what happened. I remember getting rewarded with money for perfect grades. However, my interpretation that my parents expected perfection was inaccurate. That was the story I told myself to make sense of my experience.

In a similar way, the lens of *curiosity* is just as powerful. It disarms our tendency to blame and apply judgment, especially to ourselves. Opposing labels like right and wrong, good and bad can provide simplicity to experiences that feel overwhelming or complicated. However, they also carry a weight of judgment that we use to internalize those qualities to ourselves. For example, in my younger mind, when perfection was rewarded as good, I began to believe that when I was imperfect, I was bad. The labels of "perfect" and "imperfect" became the scale I used to judge if I was worthy to receive love.

Another reason we tend to neglect applying honesty and curiosity to ourselves is that it is hard work! It feels vulnerable to open ourselves up to reexamine the challenging moments in our lives. When we are weary of struggling and feel like we are barely holding on, the last thing we want to do is open our wounds up even wider. There will be tears. We will be tempted to do acrobatic feats of nimbleness to avoid the hurt. What happens if we learn we were wrong? Fear can attach itself to what is unknown. I know because I have done this!

As uncomfortable as this might be, I promise you these tools will also allow you to let go of some of the weight and baggage you have been carrying far beyond its usefulness. Cleaning up the wounds with the antiseptic of honesty and treating them with the healing balm of curiosity allows a new story to emerge. As we move away from blame and "playing the victim" within our own story, we move into a space of ownership and empowerment.

You are more than the things that have happened to you. Your circumstances do not dictate your worth. Freedom is found as you let go of who you thought you were, acknowledge where you are right now, and begin to take steps toward remembering who you truly are in all your brilliance and power.

CHAPTER 3

DESTINATION: YOU

O ne of the most courageous things I have ever done in my life was to clear my schedule for myself. The panic attack that stopped me in my tracks let me know without a doubt that something needed to change. The life I was living was unsustainable; it was literally killing me. My stress responses were at an all-time high which meant my body was continually stuck in my fight-or-flight response. Something had to change.

Moving from survival mode into thriving takes time. In order for me to take that first step, I had to give myself time. When it became clear that I needed both time and space to figure out what was happening, I cleared my calendar. Not just for one day. Not just for one week. I canceled everything for five weeks.

I have never done that before in my life.

My calendar was where all my obligations and tasks lived. It was the measure of how my day went. Did I make it to all my appointments? Did I tick some boxes off the to-do list? Did I do enough today so that I could just do it all again tomorrow?

Prior to the panic attack, I couldn't imagine doing such a thing. My primary objective each day was to move forward and do something. Take away my calendar and what purpose did I have?

None of that mattered now. I came face-to-face with the reality that by meeting my obligations, by helping to care for everyone else, by focusing on the to-do lists to keep me moving, I had lost all sense of what made me, me. How could I continue in a life where I had lost sight of who I was? My opinions, my dreams, my personality… I was detached from all of it.

So, I canceled everything on my calendar for five weeks and decided that if I needed more time, I would give that to myself as well. I drove to my home state of California, to camp in the place I last remembered being fully me. The place that echoed the innocence of my childhood. The place I grew up before I learned to change myself for others. I was ready to find my way back to her.

The Youiest You You Can Be

The American author and cartoonist Dr. Seuss ingeniously used very simple language to communicate profound truths. His books playfully craft words and rhymes into imaginative characters and stories to illustrate the importance of the environment, the community, and respect for all people. In that spirit, The Selah Journey is a pathway for you to rediscover the wonder and per-fection of the youiest you that ever has been and ever will be. A curious, creative, contemplative way to remember how to be you. It is simple and complex all at once; easy and challenging at the same time. Take heart, my friend, as we consider the impor-tance of the destination of you.

There is only one You. Only one. You have been crafted and designed by Creator to be a perfectly unique individual in this world at this time. Read that again and let that sink in.

You belong. You are part of humanity. As a member of this worldwide association, we are not the same without you, and you are not the same without us. Even though there are times we crave our own space and solitude (believe me, as an introvert, I need alone time like I need air to breathe), it is within our connections with one another that the abundant joy in life shines.

Imagine for a moment that everyone in your life was the same. You all liked the same foods, wore the same clothes, agreed on all decisions, and liked the same music. While the harmony it creates might be desirable for a moment, it would soon become incredibly boring. The monotony of the sameness drains the color from life. Much like having a coloring book but being forced to choose only one color to use. Without our different preferences, perspectives, and personalities life feels incredibly limited.

So not only is there only one you, but we also desperately need you to be the You that you are. Without you, I might not get to know a part of me that only you can bring out. Without your passion and interests, I might miss out on experiences that enhance my engagement with the world. Without you, I might not be challenged to grow outside of my own comfortable thoughts and experiences into deeper truths and maturing realities.

Recently, I moved to Abu Dhabi with my husband for his work. Friends of ours suggested that while we were living abroad, we should explore scuba diving. We thought that could be fun, and they connected us with a local scuba instructor Nader.

Nader loves to dive. He has logged thousands of dives, has multiple certifications, and an abundance of experience. Yes, he is qualified. Yes, he is capable. Yes, he can teach. These are all things he does well. However, it is his passion and love for the experience of diving and the underwater world that sets him apart. When you watch him open up the underwater world to others and they begin to experience the joy of diving, you see his whole being shine from the inside out.

With that, Nader and I are as different as different can be. He is from the Middle East; I am from America. He is a single guy; I am a married woman. Arabic is his first language; English is my first language. He is a Muslim and I am a Christian. He has spent thousands of hours breathing and working underwater; I have spent thousands of hours listening to and mentoring others. We have come from very different cultures, religions, environments, careers, and families. But it is our very differences that allow us to grow one another.

The passion and joy Nader has for diving is infectious. His enthusiasm caused my husband and me to catch the scuba bug. Seeing the underwater world through his eyes and under his experienced care has opened up a new world of colors and life in an environment that has become a source of peace and joy for me. Additionally, I have been challenged to become a better learner by remembering how to submit to his wisdom and experience, trusting him with my life (literally!) as I learn to navigate the underwater world in which I am the alien. Likewise, my passion and joy for seeing others grow and thrive has allowed me to speak words of wisdom and self-care into his being. He is learning to trust me as a friend and guide who would love nothing

"We desperately need you to be the You that you are."

more than to see him succeed and thrive. He has brought out the scuba diver in me, bringing great joy, and I, in turn, have shared words of challenge and insight with him for improved self-care so he can keep doing what he loves. As we engage one another from our aligned and passionate individual selves, we mutually benefit.

Becoming Whole and Aligned

We are beautifully multifaceted beings who are all together greater than the sum of our parts. In my experience as a mentor, teacher, and life coach, utilizing tools like personality inventories, aptitude tests, and strengths assessments are all part of my toolkit. As you already know, I'm a big fan of anything that can help us to understand ourselves better! These are fantastic tools for what they do, but each only gives us a limited and incomplete glimpse of who we are and who we can become. For our purposes, these types of assessments are your personal signature as you engage with life. With The Selah Journey, before we explore our uniqueness, we want to focus on the big picture of who we are as whole beings.

One of my favorite frameworks as we explore our humanity and transformation is the head, heart, and hands model. This model recognizes three dynamic and interrelated components of who we are that together shape our beliefs and values: our heads, our hearts, and our hands. It also helps to illustrate how we can become off-balance if we neglect one part of the triad. All three working in harmony and connection is ideal. In order to do that, we need to consider a few things.

Head, Heart, and Hands

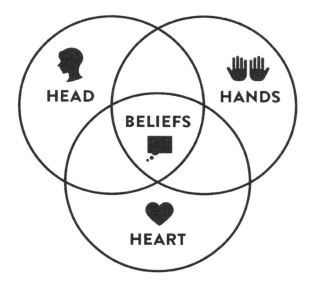

Head: This is our thinking self. It represents our intellect, knowledge, and logic.

Heart: This is our feeling self. It represents our emotions, will, and energy.

Hands: This is our doing self. It represents our actions, skills, and physicality.

First, understand that we all naturally prefer and default to one of the three. Let's imagine three of us coming together to build a birdhouse. Our "head" person might start by drawing a diagram and making a list of the supplies and tools we need. The "heart" person might start by highlighting the importance of the birdhouse being safe and attractive to the birds to keep them safe and thriving as they nest. The "hands" person will grab the supplies and start building to see what fits together naturally and how they can build a birdhouse with what they have on hand. Here's the rub: they are all correct in their approach. Is there one that seems most right to you or that you resemble more than the others? If so, that is likely your natural preference.

In the above example, we can see how all are beneficial. Considering the purpose and feel of the birdhouse helps us determine what pattern will be most effective. Taking a moment to plan before we work will help us be more efficient. Experimenting with the supplies and tools can help us visualize what the concept suggests. All three people working together will build a fantastic birdhouse. But what happens if we leave one out?

When the head and the heart work together, but the hands are left out, we can expect that the planning and concept will be on point, but the execution of actually building the birdhouse is lacking. If the heart and hands work together but leave out the head, there may be a lot of activity and good intentions along with wasted supplies and time from a trial-and-error approach. If the hands and the head work together but neglect the heart, we would likely have a functional and accurate birdhouse not suited for the birds' purposes.

This exaggerated birdhouse example illustrates that optimally all three dynamics, head, heart, and hands, are meant to work together. Now instead of three people, imagine these dynamics at work within yourself. Each of us has a default setting so to speak. This is the one we lead with. For example, I know I lead with my heart. When my head works together with my heart I am in the flow. My creative side and strategy side come together to create content, programs, and motivation. However, if my actions are not applied to this creative wave, all these great ideas stay in concept form. (This happens to me all the time!) Or, if my heart's desires and the activity of my hands partner up, I can create some colorful and fun products! But without my strategic mind engaged in the process, I skip steps, create unnecessary work, make purposeless creations, and usually, a bit of a mess for myself. And what happens when my mind and actions align, but my heart isn't in it? I can get the job done, but the passion is missing. All that results is a task completed. Nothing more. It feels like busywork, with none of the meaning or purpose.

Not only do our heads, hearts, and hands thrive when aligned, but when we desire to bring change into our lives, if we align two areas together, the third will follow. Let me explain. When I began my Selah Journey, it became obvious that the destructive and negative beliefs I held about myself from my history with depression were roadblocks to my imagining I had any worth or value. In my experience with depression, my head told me I wasn't valued, my heart felt rejection by others, and my actions seemed useless and lacking. In reality, none of these conclusions were true and accurate, but I believed I was worthless because all three of these dynamic components were aligned and communicating one message—I was worthless.

As my trusted Selah Tribe listened to me express my frustration, confusion, and grief, they challenged the destructive story in my mind that I had no worth or value to others. Repeatedly, they corrected me in love and kindness until I began to consider that if they weren't lying to me, then maybe my belief was faulty. So, what did I need to do? I needed to replace the false narrative in my head with a new one. In this case, I used my head and my hands to get my heart into alignment with the truth. To bring my thinking into alignment with a new story—I am worthy—I returned to my spiritual foundation and reminded myself that I was created by a loving Creator. I utilized a daily affirmation practice of writing and speaking out the statement, "I am worthy." I reminded myself of my friends' words whenever the old story popped up in my thoughts. I took action by investing money for myself by purchasing a personalized set of affirmation rings. I could then wear my affirmations by stacking the rings to say "I am…worthy, whole, …" etc., depending on what message I needed most that day.

Over time, the affirmations, the reminders from my friends and my faith, and the practice of wearing my rings allowed my heart to believe that maybe, just maybe, I was worthy. I tentatively embraced the truth that I am worthy. Today, I confidently affirm not only my own worthiness of love, respect, and kindness but also emphatically remind others of this truth in their own lives.

The sweet spot is found in the alignment of your head, your hands, and your heart. It is in that place your values and beliefs become embodied and solidified in your life. It is the place where your whole being is working together to engage with the life you have been given. It is where who you are and what you do flow together almost effortlessly. It is how we were designed to thrive.

Two Worlds in One

Another consideration of embracing our whole selves requires that we take a step into the quantum world. What if I told you that in you, two realities intersect and you fully belong to both? Crazy, right? But it's true! Before you roll your eyes at me and write me off as someone lost in woo-woo land, give me a chance to explain.

Let's start off with the obvious. You are a physical being. You have a physical body and exist within a physical world. You are subject to the laws of Newtonian physics, like the laws of gravity or inertia. As physical beings, we require food, water, rest, and shelter. Other physical objects affect us. We stub our toes on coffee tables and it hurts, we trip on uneven ground and fall, and we feel cold in snowy weather or warm on tropical beaches. Most of our communication with others involves body language and even some physical touch. You are a physical being, and that is foundational to who you are.

You are also an energetic being. The neural centers in your body—your brain, your heart, and your gut—also create an energetic signature that extends off your body in proportion to the strength of your energetic system. Science has mapped the energetic extension of your brain and can see that it extends approximately two inches (five centimeters) around your head. Even more incredibly, the neural network of your heart emits an energetic field that can be verified to extend from three feet (one meter) to five miles (eight kilometers) around your body, with further evidence that it may extend far beyond these distances as well. I find this absolutely fascinating...but what does this mean? Just as our physical bodies obey the laws of Newtonian physics (the realm of everything bigger than an atom), our energetic bodies follow the laws of quantum physics (the realm of atoms and smaller particles).

In you, the quantum world and the physical world meet. You are made of both atoms and photons. You fully belong to both

In you, the quantum world and the physical world meet.

worlds. You engage and operate within the laws of both worlds, even if we can't fully explain or understand what all of those laws are. We were subject to gravity before Newton scientifically explored it. Likewise, we are subject to the law of energetic waves and vibrations even as quantum physics is growing to understand exactly how these laws operate.

To make this a little more tangible, think of the practice of acupuncture. In ancient Chinese medicine, acupuncture has been around for many centuries. It works off the concept that the body has channels or meridians of energy. By engaging these meridians with thin needles along a particular meridian pattern, traditional Chinese medicine seeks to release energy blockages and restore balance within our energetic systems. This rebalancing affects our physical bodies. While science is still exploring how this works, many people have experienced the benefits of acupuncture in addressing a variety of physical, mental, and spiritual conditions. In my own experience with acupuncture, I have experienced relief and healing with symptoms of fatigue, congestion, muscle spasms, inflammation, and sciatica. We will explore this reality of our "energetic self" more in the chapters to come. For now, just marvel at what an amazing being you are!

NERD NOOK:
YOUR TOROIDAL FIELD
OF YOUR HEART

I first learned about the reality of our energetic body as I became educated about intuition. I was fascinated. To begin, let me describe for all of us non-sciency folks what makes up our energetic body.

Our nervous system generates electricity. In our bodies, we have three concentrations of neurons (cells that send and receive electronic messages) found in our brain, our heart, and our gut. These three areas effectively forming centers of "brain" activity are connected by the vagus nerve, which we referenced in the Nerd Nook in the previous chapter. As a highway of information is passed through this system, the electricity of these brain centers creates a donut-shaped magnetic field that surrounds our body. This is called a toroidal field.

We are used to assuming our brain is the most powerful electronic center in our body, but that isn't exactly true. It turns out that the heart emits a much more powerful electromagnetic field for our bodies. Additionally, the quality of the heart (toroidal) field is affected by our emotional energy as well. Why is this important?

Our toroidal field is energetically reading and communicating with others and our world at all times. Developing a state of coherence within our physical and energetic self affects the quality of our connections with others and the world. Coherence is achieved when the energetic force of our mind, heart, gut, emotion, and action are aligned in a harmonious rhythm. When we hold conflicting or disruptive thoughts, our congruence decreases. When we experience emotions related to anger, fear, or sadness, our congruence is disrupted. Fostering positive emotions like compassion and peace elevates our congruence. When our thoughts and emotions work together for our good, our congruence is greater.

And this is all interconnected with our body through that vagus nerve. Yep! That same nerve that regulates our fight, flight, freeze, and calm states of being. While this is just an introduction to help us understand how intricately our physical and energetic beings are intertwined, I invite you to follow me down the rabbit hole into the very real world of intuition and energy. It will expand your understanding and the way you choose to show up in the world.

Becoming the Future You

Envision a map opened up before you. The "You Are Here" is your starting place. All around this spot are the map symbols that indicate your terrain. Icons of the past you have carried with you up to this moment, the stories you have relied upon to get you here, the pain points you endure as travel wounds, the instability and chaos that fuels your doubt and mistrust, and the baggage you have packed away but have not found the energy or time to go through it, and lighten your load. And then you follow a highlighted path, the plan to get from "You Are Here" to your Destination.

You are that Destination. You: body, soul, and spirit. You: head, heart, and hands. You: embodied and energetic. Can you see her, standing at your destination, encouraging you to take the first step? What does she look like? What do you see that calls you forward and motivates you to take the next step toward becoming her? How does she feel? What is her mood, her emotions? She is you, thriving and whole, a full expression of your unique personality, talents, passions, values, and purpose. She is the youiest you you can be.

The pathway between the You right now and this future You is your Selah Journey. As you travel this road, it will be imperative that you keep your eyes on the destination ahead. Why? Because you are in charge. You get to choose where this path leads. You are in the driver's seat, and you control the direction and pace of this journey. You choose the next step, the next turn, the next detour, the next vista.

As you take the journey, pay attention to the insights and possibilities this future holds out for you. What dreams begin to take form in your heart? What visions start unfolding as you travel? What intentions do you hold as you move forward? It is all part of your becoming a fuller and more authentic version of yourself. A truer you.

But Cami... (I can hear you thinking this) ... this sounds so positive, so easy, so optimistic. You don't know what I've gone through. You don't know what I'm carrying. You don't know how weary I am. I'm not even sure if I believe this is possible. I've been hopeful before, and it has hurt me. I don't know if I have the energy or ability to try one more time.

To this, I can say, you are right. I do not know the specifics of your "You Are Here." I do not know how many times you have dared to hope for something better and have been met with disappointment. I do not know what you are carrying. I do remember my own past and feeling as if I was in an ocean of waves crashing over me again and again. I felt so overwhelmed and couldn't catch a breath between the waves that kept forcing me under the water. Was it even worth trying to catch a break? Catch a breath? Somewhere, in the midst of me just trying to survive, a friend suggested I was worth it. I didn't believe it the first time they said it, or the second time, or the time after that. Eventually, though, a small glimmer of "maybe" appeared. Maybe I was worth the effort. Maybe I could survive. Maybe one day not only would I survive, but I might even attain something resembling average and boring.

Let me be that friend for you today. You are worth it. You matter. Your circumstances do not dictate your value. You are unique: one-of-a-kind. You belong. I know it with every atom and photon of my being. Not only that, but as you courageously choose to believe this and take steps toward that future you, you will bring hope and joy and love to yourself and those around you. Take heart, precious friend. Dream your dreams, because they are yours to embrace and share with the world.

Follow your Selah Journey and find the freedom to be exactly who you are.

The

PRACTICE

CHAPTER 4

SABBATH RESTING

When I remember back to my first Selah Journey, my lifelong friend, Brooks, looked me straight in the eyes and bluntly observed, "You need to sleep." Sometimes we are blind to what is so obvious to others. He spoke the truth, and I needed to hear his wisdom.

For at least a decade, I had been operating in a kind of survival mode. Not only was I in a lengthy season of depression (with bouts of insomnia sprinkled in for good measure), but it seemed like major life stresses came rolling through me like waves pounding against the beach, one after the other. I was a working mom, living where I worked. My kids needed me, my work needed me. My extended family was moving through a series of health scares and a massive natural disaster that took their homes, jobs, and communities. My lack of boundaries and haphazard self-care practices kept me feeling like I could not let go of any aspect of my life for fear it would fall apart. I was searching for my purpose while taking on the responsibility for everything and everyone in my life. With each new wave, I felt more and more worn down.

When I arrived in California, I was camping where our family home used to stand before a wildfire erased it from our lives. The land was recovering, as well as the wildlife. In my exhaustion, the fear of being surprised by a bear or mountain lion kept me on alert. (The worst that actually happened was a slightly perturbed deer stamping outside my tent, once, then left.) So, when Brooks bluntly stated, "You need to sleep," he was right on many levels. I had neglected rest, wearing my busy schedule and lack of sleep like a medal of honor. I had been a fool.

All parts of me needed rest. My body had forgotten how to fall asleep. Years of demanding it to be constantly at the ready had left my body stuck in the "on" position. My mind felt frantic, craving the stability of routine and rhythm. My emotions were numb, having been ignored and shoved down because I told myself my opinions didn't matter. My spirit was stifled, as I felt distant from my faith and purpose. I needed to sleep.

It took about a year from that encounter for me to get all the pieces in place. I began to work with a sleep doctor, who revealed physical issues that kept my body in a continual state of alertness. I worked with another medical practitioner who helped me find the mental support I needed to fall asleep. I learned to protect eight hours for sleep daily and reminded myself that sleep deprivation was negatively affecting every aspect of my life. I began my journey into rest with steps to improve my physical sleep. Soon thereafter, the rest of my being desired to follow suit.

"You are a human-being, not a human-doing."

Sleep Is Essential

In the opening chapter of Matthew Walker's book, *Why We Sleep: The New Science of Sleep and Dreams*, he states that "emerging from this [sleep] research renaissance is an unequivocal message: sleep is the single most effective thing we can do to reset our brain and our body health each day—Mother Nature's best effort yet at contra-death." Lack of sleep is equivalent to a lack of water; we can only survive so long without it. Incredibly, even a small lack of sleep has far-reaching effects on our bodies and our minds.

I did my best to act as if I was the exception to this fact for about twenty years or so. I sacrificed sleep so I could be available for others, allowing my sleep deficit to grow into a mountain of debt while I balanced my dual careers of motherhood and resident director. My dad had a note saying, "You can't soar with the eagles in the morning if you hoot with the owls all night." Well, I tried to do both for far too long. Before the panic attack that prompted my Selah Journey, I was struggling on all fronts. Physically, I struggled with systemic inflammation, obesity, and insomnia. Mentally, I saw my life as an endless checklist. Emotionally, I had numbed my feelings to quiet them. Spiritually, I felt lost and disconnected from Creator. My lack of sleep was a significant contributing factor to all of my struggles.

So, what do we gain by sleeping? When you begin to dig into the science and study of sleep, the impact is fascinating. Presenting you with the list of benefits and improvements sounds like a too-good-to-be-true advertisement of a magic elixir. For now, let's consider it from our head, heart, and hands framework.

Sleep and Our Thinking Self

Sleep has a powerful impact on our mind's capacity for learning, memory, and attentiveness. Walker uses the analogy of a memory stick to help us understand what happens in our brains when we sleep. Each day, the "memory stick" (a.k.a., the short-term memory center of your brain) collects thoughts, knowledge, facts, and details from your day. That evening, as you sleep, your brain moves all that information from the "memory stick" into long-term "filing" and categorizes it for easy access. When our bodies get the recommended seven to nine hours of restful and refreshing sleep, this transfer of information happens brilliantly, and your "memory stick" will be fully cleared and prepared for the next day's opportunities and insights. However, when our quantity and quality of sleep are reduced, even by just an hour or so, all aspects of this process are diminished. The knowledge transfer from the memory stick into our long-term mental files is incomplete and some of the information gets stuck in our short-term memory center. The "memory stick" also loses some of its capability and efficiency as it holds onto the partial information from the day before, and the long-term "filing" is incomplete and messy. Eventually, our memory system looks like an extremely disorganized desk! Our ability to store, access, and use information on a daily basis hinges on sleeping eight hours every night.

Our mental attentiveness is also affected by our quality of sleep more than you might think. For comparison, let's consider how driving under the influence of alcohol (or drugs) affects us. Alcohol impairs our judgment, slows our responses, and physiologically makes us less attentive. Countries around the world regulate how much alcohol one can consume before you are too compromised to drive, with some countries enforcing zero-percent tolerance laws. Why is that? Because our judgment, responsiveness, and attentiveness are essential for us to be able to drive a car safely. Studies are now showing that sleep deprivation affects our mental capacity for driving the same way that alcohol does. Our attentiveness and mental capacity decrease after fifteen hours of wakefulness, according to one study from Australia. So, if you wake up at 7:00 a.m., by 10:00 p.m. your brain function begins to diminish. And if you are still awake by 2:00 a.m., you are functioning at the same capacity as someone who is legally too drunk to drive in the United States! In short, our brains need sleep to function. Like any finely tuned system, when we provide what our brains and bodies need, our mental capacity can thrive! And when it comes to sleep, even small deficits have big impacts.

Sleep and Our Embodied Self

Walker asserts that sleep is absolutely foundational for good health, more so than even a healthy diet and exercise. He even provides the science to support his claim. To understand this more fully, let's consider just one way in which this is true for our bodies. Remember when we discussed our vagus nerve in a previous Nerd Nook? That is the nerve that connects our three brains to one another and communicates to our bodies if we need to have our fight, flight, or freeze responses activated. When we carry a sleep deficit, this system gets stuck in activation mode far beyond what is actually needed. When we are revved up in this survival response for extended periods of time, it is really punishing on our entire body. Just like keeping a racing car revved up all the time, the wear and tear to our body builds up more quickly and we end up requiring more frequent and attentive maintenance. Sleep deprivation is one source of continual elevated stress which contributes to altered hormones, an overtaxed cardiovascular system, and an unbalanced metabolism.

Not only is sleep required to keep our bodies' physical functioning within an optimal range, sleep is also foundational for a robust immune system. When we sleep, our bodies heal. Rest is necessary to keep our immune system running smoothly and fully stocked. As just one example, did you know that our immune system contains a natural killer cell that seeks and destroys foreign elements (like cancer) in our system? A California study showed that with just one "bad night" of four hours of sleep, we lose 70% of our natural killer cells. In a world where it can feel like our bodies are constantly fighting off sickness and infections, we can't afford to deplete our immune system so drastically! The World Health Organization has even identified working a nighttime shift as a probable carcinogen because the disrupted sleep it can cause has such a big impact on our immune system. Being sick and tired of being sick and tired only has one cure... sleep.

Sleep and Our Feeling Self

Have you noticed that when you are sleep-deprived, you have less control over your emotions? You can "lose" your verbal filter by saying things you might otherwise hold back or lashing out in a more powerful way than is typical for you. That is because lack of sleep disrupts the balance between the logical center of our brain and the emotional processing center of our brain.

It also amplifies the response of your emotional center so you feel things more intensely and with less ability to navigate your strong feelings.

Insomnia often goes hand in hand with many forms of mental health issues, such as chronic depression, bipolar disorder, and addiction disorders. In fact, all psychiatric conditions are connected with some form of abnormal sleep. Clearly, healthy sleep and healthy emotions go hand in hand. By no means am I trying to oversimplify the very complex and interrelated issues of mental health, but I am trying to highlight a foundational correlation. If we can improve our quality of sleep, we can improve our emotional health. Anecdotally, since I began my Selah Journey and have prioritized my sleep health, my mental health has become much more manageable. Quality sleep was not the only factor that eased my chronic depression, but it was a critical factor.

NERD NOOK:
THE NREM AND REM SLEEP DANCE

We have explored some of the effects sleep has on us and hopefully, we are growing in our understanding of why that is important. But my inner nerd wants to know a little bit more about how it works and why eight hours is the magic number. When we begin to grasp how sleep is utilized in the brain, the cycle of non-rapid eye movement (NREM) sleep and rapid eye movement (REM) sleep provides an interesting story.

First, what are NREM and REM sleep and how do they differ from one another? If we were to map our brainwaves from awake to asleep, we would see a progression from: 1) highly active and chaotic brain activity in various centers in our brain (awake); to 2) similar brain activity while we are unconscious, unmoving, and dreaming, which also is identified by rapid eye movements under our closed eyelids (REM sleep); and finally 3) a deepening progression of much slower and coordinated brain activity, similar to meditation, that washes through our entire brain from front to back (NREM sleep). NREM sleep progresses in four stages from light to deep sleep as it becomes harder to wake us up as this stage of sleep continues.

As we slumber, our brains experience a dance between our REM and NREM sleep approximately every ninety minutes. During our first couple of dance cycles, we spend more time in deep NREM sleep and very little in REM sleep. Studies suggest that at this time of our evening, the NREM sleep is tidying up and removing unnecessary neural connections, preparing the long-term storage space for the incoming information from our "memory stick" for the day. Then as sleep continues, each ninety-minute cycle uses less NREM sleep and transitions to more REM sleep. It is in REM that our brain strengthens our neural connections and integrates our memories and information cohesively into our brain.

So, throughout the evening, our brain progresses through five sleep cycles in eight hours. First, it prepares for all the incoming data we receive during the day. Then it begins to transfer and organize the information to the appropriate centers of our brain. Finally, it cohesively integrates all that data with meaning as we dream. Since each cycle moves us through this dance as the evening marches on, if we miss out on an hour or two, the dance is altered. If we go to bed later than our norm, we miss out on the opening dance cycle and miss out on some of the preparatory NREM sleep that opens up space for new memories and info. If we wake up earlier than our norm, we interrupt the integration activity of our REM sleep, robbing ourselves of new connections and insights we gain during integration.

The more I learn the processes and importance of sleep, the more passionate I become about protecting it in my life. Our brains are amazingly complex and integrated, coordinating all our physical, mental, and emotional abilities and processes. Sleep is absolutely foundational for a healthy life. I will be the first in line to cheer you on as you take steps to prioritize and protect the physical rest you need.

Beyond Sleep Towards Wholistic Rest

My journey of understanding the importance of rest actually began decades before my Selah Journey. You see, throughout my college career, I was a committed overachiever. My identity was anchored to high grades and an overfull schedule. I embodied an ability to overcommit to activities and somehow do it all and do it all well. Unaware of the imbalance this lifestyle was creating, I convinced myself that the stress I created in my week helped me focus and provided me with the motivation to succeed.

Entering one particular week, I was feeling significantly overwhelmed. My religious convictions justified my schedule because I told myself that all these commitments were ultimately to glorify Creator; therefore, S/He would help me achieve all my tasks, assignments, and appointments. However, my left brain could not figure out how this was possible. In exasperation, I prayed out to Spirit, lamenting that I had to sleep and that there were only twenty-four hours in a day. I had so much to do! Couldn't S/He help me by giving me more hours or reducing my need for rest?

Spirit has a sense of humor. No sooner had I finished my spiritual plea, but I heard a voice in my head respond with a solution. "Take a Sabbath," it insisted.

"Very funny, Spirit. You didn't hear me correctly. I was asking for more time in my week, not less. If I can't finish my commitments in the seven days you have already given me, how can I possibly do it in six? You have got to be kidding! Take a whole day off? Impossible!"

"Take a Sabbath." The voice insisted.

I quickly learned that when Creator gives you an answer, S/He does not change Their mind. You can ask again, question, argue, and negotiate but no matter your plea, Spirit is steadfast.

Take a Sabbath. What does that even mean? The Jewish tradition observes a time of no "work" from sundown on Friday evening to Saturday evening. That was the first idea that came to mind. So, what did that mean for me? A twenty-four-hour pause in my week? Hmmm, a full day of rest. While my logical brain had absolutely no way of comprehending this conundrum, I committed to heeding Creator's advice and giving Sabbath a try. What I was currently doing wasn't working, and I knew it was no use arguing with Them. I rearranged my schedule and blocked off that Sunday as a day of no work. What did "no work" mean? For me, my work at that time was school, so I decided to commit to no assignments, papers, or study groups. If I couldn't work for a day, what could I do? I decided that I could say yes to church, worship, friends, and rest. With my guidelines identified and my day blocked off, the Sabbath experiment began.

It was hard work! I had to work a bit harder on Monday through Saturday to be prepared for the next week so that I wouldn't be tempted to cheat on my Sabbath day. I also changed the daily rhythm since I could sleep later and say yes to more social time. It felt uncomfortable not to be driven by my planner or a to-do list. It was my first taste at another way of being present in my life and it prompted some fear and anxiety, to be honest. If I wasn't achieving anything that day, what did that say about my value as a human? Did I deserve this day of rest? What if I had forgotten something important and let someone else down?

*"Sabbath Resting
is freedom
from striving,
and freedom
toward thriving."*

After the experiment of my first Sabbath was over, I noticed something I hadn't anticipated. I felt more present in my life. Since my time to work was more limited than in past weeks, I was able to prioritize my assignments and tasks more efficiently and let go of some that were less important. Surprisingly, it worked! Creator was right! (Of course, S/He was!) I didn't need more days in the week or fewer hours of sleep. What I needed was a better rhythm that demanded I prioritize what was most important. I needed to be introduced to a way to be in the world that did not require me to do something in order to be valued.

A weekly Sabbath became a rhythm I started to incorporate into every week. Was I perfect at it? No. Not even close. But the more I practiced a Sabbath, the more I craved it. It was counterintuitive to my young adult mind, but I began to realize that by removing twenty-four hours from my work week I gained something much more in return. I gained a bit of balance in my rhythm. I gained a new perspective that helped me prioritize my commitments in a healthier way. I gained a step towards better self-care practices that I now understand are foundational in my life. And, I gained deeper connections with Creator, within myself, and with my family and friends.

Ever since then, my starting point for rest begins with the concept of the Sabbath. Building upon physical rest, the Sabbath encourages me to consider rest from a holistic framework. Sabbath Resting embraces a different way of being in the world. Although I first became aware of the concept of the Sabbath in my Judeo-Christian studies, many religions and philosophies encourage a rhythm of rest. The Jewish theologian Abraham Joshua Heschel describes the Sabbath as a taste of what is to come saying: "Six days a week we wrestle with the world, wringing profit from the earth; on the Sabbath we especially care for the seed of eternity planted in the soul. The world has our hands, but our soul belongs to Someone Else." The Buddhist practice observes Uposatha or a time of renewal each lunar month. Buddhist monk and teacher Thich Nhat Hanh has said, "Our body and mind have the capacity to heal themselves if we allow them to rest. Stopping, calming, and resting are preconditions for healing. If we cannot stop, the course of our destruction will just continue." Rhythmic, holistic rest is beneficial to humanity. This truth is reflected throughout a multitude of practices and traditions around the globe. Your responsibility is to understand, from your own beliefs, what it means for you. How do you enact this in your own life? As I have explored this practice throughout my life, albeit haphazardly, it has come to represent a time of freedom for me.

What do I mean by freedom? When the word "freedom" is used it is understood in two ways—freedom from, and freedom to. When we look at what we want freedom from, we begin to identify the aspects of our lives that feel confining, limiting, or heavy. Maybe it is a circumstance you find yourself in or a mindset that keeps tripping you up. Maybe it is an overloaded schedule or an endless to-do list that makes it difficult to find a moment for yourself. During my first sabbath experiment, I was seeking freedom from the work of school because the list of assignments and meetings felt endless. During my first Selah Journey, I was seeking freedom from an overloaded schedule with a tower of to-do items, most of which were for others. What we seek freedom from will change throughout our lives, depending on our roles, attitudes, and circumstances. No matter your season of life, there is always room to grow. Identifying what you want freedom from is a great question to be curious about.

We also view freedom from the vantage point of what we are free to move towards. Shifting from what we want to be released from into what we want to embrace illuminates our passions and highlights what we increasingly crave in our life. Freedom allows us to expand and step towards a more vibrant and aligned version of ourselves. Again, when I was in college, having a day free from assignments and meetings was refreshing. I was free to invest more in my friendships and my faith. During my first Selah Journey, I freed myself from exterior obligations and freed myself to listen to my soul and ground myself in truths. When we think of Sabbath Resting, consider finding a rhythmic time of setting aside (just for a bit) what you must do, and allowing in more of what lifts and inspires you. For me, it is my "Get To, not, Have To" day: freedom from striving, and freedom toward thriving.

Holding Space

All this may sound incredible, but when you are wading through the pressures of life, and all the responsibilities and all the expectations of the daily grind tug you in every which way, Sabbath Resting probably feels unattainable. Incredible, but out of reach. How can you find rest when life doesn't stop? How can you find space within a rhythm that accommodates everyone else in your life but you? Let's see if we can look at this from a different perspective.

I'm an avid reader. As a kid, I would devour books. Once, I ran out of books to read so I grabbed the encyclopedia set belonging to my parents and started reading, one by one. (If you don't know what an encyclopedia is, ask your grandmother!) I also used to hide a flashlight in my bed and shine it under the covers to join Nancy Drew as she solved each mystery within the pages of those yellow hardcover books. Even now, when I'm on the go, I typically have something to read in my backpack or purse, just in case I have a few minutes to duck into a coffee shop and lose myself in an epic saga or glean wisdom from another's experience. Inevitably, though, the time comes to return to the real world and I slip a bookmark into the pages, pausing the action until I return to it.

A pause in the action. Sabbath Resting is your bookmark. It is the pause in the everyday march of life. It is the commitment to carry your bookmark with you, and at the appointed times and places, use it to hold a little space for yourself. Just like my reading addiction where I am continually looking to steal a few moments to return to the captivating pages of my books, Sabbath Resting is like carrying your own personalized bookmark of self-care with you everywhere you go. And either when the opportunity presents itself, or better yet, when you reach the protected pause in your day, you take your bookmark out of your schedule, hang it up for all to see, and enter into the sacred, life-giving space that is all about you.

Sabbath Resting is also beautifully wholistic. Just as physical rest is vital for our well-being, so is mental, emotional, social, and spiritual rest. Explore this for a minute with me. What does protecting your resting space in these different facets of life look like for you? What activities (or non-activities) feel restorative for you? To prime your creative juices, allow me to share some of my favorite Sabbath Resting activities:

- A solo drive on dirt roads through the mountains of Colorado. (Social rest—introvert time to recharge my battery; mental rest—being immersed in nature instead of my to-do list.)
- A warm mug of cocoa, curled up with a book, in front of a fireplace in the winter. (Mental rest—a book to give my brain something different to focus on; social rest—more cozy introvert time.)
- Taking a walk and listening to music that fits my mood. (Emotional rest—the outlet of activity and music to release my backlog of emotions.)
- Catching up with a friend via Zoom or meeting them face-to-face. (Emotional rest—connecting and being seen by those people who are in my corner.)
- Family movie night. (Mental rest—a movie to engage my mind; emotional rest—creating a positive and relaxed moment of connection with my family.)
- Meditation and/or prayer time. (Spiritual rest—connecting with my source, drawing in whatever my spirit needs; emotional rest—releasing what has burdened my heart.)

Like any new practice, starting is the hardest and most important part. It can look like setting aside an entire day, as I did in college with my first Sabbath Resting experiment, or it can look like smaller protected blocks of time within your daily rhythms, depending on what is needed to stay healthy within your current season of life. Maybe you develop practices that incorporate utilizing your Sabbath Resting bookmark daily, weekly, and/ or monthly. However you decide to start, I encourage you to commit to protecting some sacred space this week that honors your humanness.

And before you can say, "But, I don't have any time," or "I haven't earned it yet," or "I'm not worth it," just stop for a moment. You are a human being. You matter. You are unique and the world needs your uniqueness to be completed and perfected. My belief system is founded upon a loving Creator who formed everything, including you. And like any loving parent, this Spirit wants you to thrive and find joy. Throughout our lifetime, it is common to lose sight of the truth of who we are and think our value comes from what we do, instead of "Whose" we are. Let me remind you; you are more than what you do. You are a human being, not a "human doing." Within you resides the spark, handiwork, and connection of that which is Divine. Sabbath Resting brings us back to our worthiness by holding and protecting space for us to reconnect with the miraculous beings we are. Pull out your bookmark, take a pause within the busyness of your life, enter into your Sabbath Resting space for a moment, and just be.

CHAPTER 5

THE GIFT OF REFLECTION

Nyepi

Recently, I had the privilege of traveling to Bali for a weeklong vacation with my husband, Stefan. It was a bit of a last-minute trip and in our hasty preparations, we learned our visit would be during the Balinese New Year. What a surprise! I was excited to experience the Balinese way of celebrating the new year. As we briefly researched the experience, we learned that New Year's Day is called Nyepi, The Day of Silence.

Upon arrival, our hotel informed us that on Nyepi, we would have to stay on the property for the day while the locals practiced their day of silence. You see, in Bali, this day is one of the most sacred and important days of the entire year. The Balinese begin each new year with four prohibitions—no lights and/or fires, no work, no entertainment or pleasure, and no traveling. Some individuals also observe the additional restrictions of no talking and no eating. Everything is closed except the hospitals. Hotels just provide simple housing and food for visitors to the area.

Everything else is closed. All stores and restaurants. The airport. All roads. It is a day of complete stillness on the island.

This first day of the New Year is dedicated to meditation and reflection. There is a shared stillness as cooking fires are extinguished and sunlight is the only light used. The island and the people collectively rest and breathe deeply in preparation for the year to come. Imagine your nation encouraging and protecting a time of self-examination for all its people. A complete day to rest the resources of the land, allowing the air pollution of travel and business to dissipate, and pausing the draw on energy sources, allowing renewal for a day. (And if it is not overcast, it is the best evening to observe the stars overhead.)

But it is not just a day of rest. It is a day for contemplation, reflection, and meditation. Households stay within their homes and pay attention to their own hearts, minds, and souls. Questions probe into their being. What have you learned over the course of the past year? What are you proud of? How can you better attend to your priorities and families? Are there any wounds you need to address within yourself or with others? Can you hear the whispers of encouragement and admonitions of Spirit? What is your soul speaking to you? How are you experiencing deep joy and love in your life? Where have you wronged or hurt others, and how might you repair what has been broken?

As guests of Bali, we also embraced Nyepi. Stefan and I kept lights off or dimmed all day and only left our villa for meals. We thanked those who were working during this sacred day for their sacrifice on our behalf. We sat in curiosity and asked each other questions and talked about our plans for the future. We watched the birds and dragonflies zip around above the rice fields

"A mirror cannot show what is not there, nor ignore what is."

until a few brave stars shone bright enough to be seen amid the clouds. Although we only engaged with one day of their New Year celebrations, that one day made a great difference for us. We embraced the Gift of Reflection that Nyepi offered, and we continued to do so throughout our vacation.

Mirror, Mirror on the Wall

When I think of the act of reflection, images of mirrors immediately come to mind. My relationship with mirrors is best described as a love-hate relationship. I guess I can't hold it against them; after all, they are just a tool that reflects. How we feel about them is connected to how we use them. In my home, I have one in my entryway to allow that space to feel bigger than it truly is. I also have mirrors in some of the bedrooms in my home to capture the natural light through the windows and reflect it into the shadowed spaces. But then, there are two in my bathroom. One magnifies my face so I can apply my makeup, shape my eyebrows, or pluck the invading menopausal facial hairs on my chin. The other shows me what I look like, for better or for worse, before I step out into the world. These mirrors show me how futile it is to hide the pounds of comfort eating, the lines of exhaustion, or how a boost of confidence increases my glow. I cannot hide from the truths they reveal.

The reflection from a mirror cannot lie. (Ok… maybe at Disneyland, but you know what I mean….) It cannot show you what is not there, and it cannot ignore what is there: it reflects what is objectively true. How we respond to its reflection and the information it provides shapes our attitudes and beliefs. In a similar way, The Selah Journey's Gift of Reflection is a practice designed to help us see into ourselves in order to gain a more accurate or true understanding of who we are. It illuminates how our responses and beliefs have come into our present reality and shape our future.

Remember when I insisted that along your Selah Journey, honesty was a required traveling companion? Well, this is where she shines. Let us pause for a moment, though. What comes up for you when you think about being honest with yourself? How do your emotions shift? Do any events or memories rise to the surface? When I began to practice reflection on my first Selah Journey, my friends would remark how brave I was. Brave? I didn't feel brave, but I did feel desperate. I had reached a place in my life where my avoidance of the facts (my stress level, my lack of self-care practices, my beliefs about myself) led me to a place where I didn't want to be the main character in my own story anymore. Honesty threw me a lifeline and simply stated that if I wanted to recover what I had lost, I needed to dive into the truth of "me." So, I decided to pick up the lifeline and allow the Gift of Reflection to show me what had been there all along.

Where my friends saw bravery as I dove into the deep end of reflection, I felt fear. What if I discovered I was truly as terrible as my thoughts had shouted at me? What if I learned more about how deeply I had hurt others around me? What if I was throwing away a life that others would love to live? What if moving forward was too hard? What if? What if? What if? This is one reason why we shun honesty and truth when it comes to ourselves. Although we advise others that choosing honesty when dealing with each other is a hallmark of trustworthiness and integrity, when given the chance to refocus the mirror of honesty on ourselves, we squirm in avoidance and fear. Just like putting off going to the doctor, honesty with ourselves leads us to the truth—but what if we don't like what is revealed? We live with a double standard; honesty is the best policy with others, but ignorance is bliss when it comes to ourselves.

The truth is, if we aren't honest with ourselves and see what is truly there, we cannot move through it into transformation. What use is it for us to stay blind to the lie we have chosen to believe? Shining a light on what is false and confronting it with truth—this is honesty. We use projections, facades, and false beliefs to protect ourselves from hurt, rejection, shame, and fear. But these are powerless to dismantle the truth; they merely conceal it. Honesty requires us to move past the facade and look at what is true. And this is when things get good because then, true healing and transformation begin. To walk your Selah Journey is to walk towards thriving as your authentic self. Authenticity requires honesty.

I can't tell you what you will encounter when you allow that mirror of reflection to shine the light of honesty into your own life. Whatever it reveals, I believe it will be worth the work that will bring growth into your life, if you let it. Doubt, worry, and fear will likely become big and scary in your life before you take that first step. But whether you are brave or desperate, stepping into the Gift of Reflection with honesty is one of the best steps towards transformation you can take in your life.

Authenticity
requires
honesty.

NERD NOOK:
ST. IGNATIUS' GENIUS—
PAUSE AND THINK

To understand why the practice of reflection is so powerful, consider the historic educator and expert of transformation, Ignatius of Loyola, the founder of the Jesuit community. Through his intellectual studies and spiritual pursuits, Saint Ignatius developed a pedagogy of instruction that has become the foundation of Jesuit schools around the world. Its focal point and overall aim are the transformation of the whole individual toward action in the world, founded upon a bedrock of morality. In other words, Ignatius was passionately committed to individuals developing into authentic people equipped to do good works in the world. Can you see why I like the guy so far? This is kinda my thing too.

Seeking to educate in such a way that the student would be transformed from the inside out, Ignatius developed a paradigm that works something like this:

CONTEXT: THE PERSONS

Your thoughts, history, opinions, experiences, feelings, etc.

EVALUATION: THE PROGRESS

Context: This is the person. You. Your history, beliefs, experiences, circumstances, thoughts, emotions...all of it. You are the subject and object of the transformation process, just like you are in The Selah Journey.

Experience: With any given aspect of who you are, experiences comprise what you know or have encountered associated with that part of you. For example, in my life, my experiences with silence have shaped my thoughts and emotions. When I receive silence from someone, my first reaction is to believe they are disappointed in me or disapprove of me. This is my experience.

Reflection: Applying objective perspective and curiosity to your experiences, reflection allows you to examine your experiences for deeper understanding or insight. In my case, I might consider what memories I have of silence that taught me to associate it with anger and disappointment. Do I use silence to communicate disappointment with others, or do I use it for other reasons as well? Does silence always communicate disapproval, or might there be other explanations I was unaware of?

Action: At this point, you apply new insights, truths, or theories you gained from your reflections to your life. For example, if I have come to understand there may be other reasons for silence than disappointment, I may ask others for clarity when I feel familiar reactions rise up when someone stops communicating with me. Or, I can direct my attention to my own communication habits to improve the clarity of both my words and my silences.

Evaluation: In walking through this cycle of learning, are you progressing towards your goals? If your transformation is the goal, evaluating the process periodically allows you to celebrate your growth and identify new milestones to move toward.

The key in this whole model is The Gift of Reflection! So often we have an experience and immediately react according to how we feel. What unlocks the power of change in you is the reflection piece. We have an absolute gift in our ability to reflect on the events and emotions in our lives. Whether it is our

own practices we utilize, like journaling or meditation, or we turn to a life coach or counselor to help us
evaluate our experiences, the practice of reflection
unlocks the steps of transformation.

Attentiveness in Action

Reflection is the key to transformation, and the first aspect of
reflection is the practice of paying attention. Today, we live in
a world of distraction. Recent studies of attention span, by Gloria
Mark, PhD, suggest that our average attention span has rapidly
decreased over the last twenty years from 2.5 minutes in 2004
to 75 seconds in 2012, and only 47 seconds today. In a world
of digital screens, endless information, and idolizing efficiency
(doing more in less and less time), it is no wonder our ability
to focus has diminished. Thankfully, with practice and adjustment, we can strengthen our capacity to focus. As we do, rich
rewards await us.

My first taste of the power of attentiveness happened in the
fall of 2011. I was participating in a Soul Sabbath retreat: a day
spent in silence while paying attention to the whispers of my soul.
I have such strong memories of that day; the smell of the earth
rising up as my feet walked through the fallen leaves in the maple
grove. The warm sun on my skin and the cool earth at my back
as I lay in the grass listening to wind rustle through the remaining
leaves on the autumn bare trees. A ladybug searched along my
hand before spreading her hidden wings to fly off to a new venue.
That day passed slowly and quickly. The memories are full of
sound, smell, and vibrant colors. But what I remember most
vividly from that day were the whispers of my soul. I remember

the moment on the grassy knoll when my spirit reminded me that all I truly needed was to know I was loved deeply by Creator. No success nor failure, no weakness nor strength, no action nor attitude would ever change that truth.

That centering and grounding knowledge came from one day of being purposely attentive. A day when I allowed the past to remain in the past and the future to remain in the future while I inhabited the gift of the present moment with my whole being—head, heart, and hands. Truly, we exist only in the present moment. Attending to and taking notice of our present is the doorway to connecting with our authentic presence; our true self. The present moment is also the space in which we connect with our true source, the presence of Spirit. While we can remember the past and have hope for our future, we experience life— fullness of life—only in the present. The practice of attentive- ness allows us to receive, learn, and understand with more clarity and depth.

The truth I received on that day in 2011—I am deeply loved—has continued to resurface throughout my life in times when I forget who I am as I strive towards who I am becoming. It also returns when I remember past struggles that once held me captive to old stories I used to believe. And this is what The Gift of Reflection makes possible. Within your Selah Journey, the practice of paying attention and attending to your presence is the first step of reflection. It is in those attentive moments that we connect with the wisdom of our head, our heart, and our hands. It is from those moments we take what we have learned and practice a new way of being ourselves in the world.

More Curiosity

Not only do we travel The Selah Journey with honesty and atten-tiveness, curiosity is also a requirement. How does that work? Well, let's tease this out a bit. As we grow up, we begin to make judgments about what is right behavior and wrong behavior. As we learn what is right and wrong, we are also exercising our skill of discernment, judging between the two so that we can best choose our actions for desired results. This skill is incred-ibly important! Understanding how to act in social situations or knowing how to apply our moral compass to everyday life is vital. However, as we begin our journey into reflection, if we lead our reflection with judgment instead of curiosity, our process of transformation cannot even get started. At this stage of the journey, curiosity is a much better companion.

To illustrate, let's examine something that came up for me when I was living in the United Arab Emirates (UAE). We initially moved to Abu Dhabi for my husband's work believing we would stay for a short-term residency. As it tends to happen in the UAE, an opportunity to extend our time into a longer-term commitment arose, and we began examining our thoughts and emotions around this new offer. One of the things I noticed arising in me was a feeling of guilt. I felt that if I wanted to say yes and extend our move for another few years, I would be letting down my family back in the States. Exploring this feeling through a judgmental lens sounded something like this:

- Am I abandoning my family by choosing to stay?
- How selfish am I to even think of choosing what I want over what my family might want or need?

- Staying primarily for the money and benefits is really shallow, right?
- Extending my time in Abu Dhabi is the easy choice. But doing what is right isn't often easy.

Can you hear how my judgment-oriented thoughts shifted my process from evaluating an opportunity to questioning my character by casting me in the role of a selfish, shallow, self-centered, and lazy individual? I didn't want to be any of those things! Reflecting on feelings and thoughts from a place of judgment assigns a "right" or "wrong" answer and imposes a layer of morality on what we have noticed. This shifts the focus from "What can I learn or discover from this feeling?" (self-discovery), to "How might my decision impact how others see me?" (ego-protection). Now, how does this change if I lean into curiosity instead of judgment? Examining my feelings sounded more like this:

- I wonder where this feeling came from?
- What can I learn from this feeling?
- Is this accurate? Would they actually feel this way? If so, how might that affect my decision?
- When have I felt like this before? What did I learn from that experience?

Can you feel how those questions shifted me in different directions? The first set of questions revealed my fear of how others might label my potential choice to stay as bad, wrong, or morally lacking. The second set of questions allowed me to move into the origin of that feeling and listen more closely to where I was experiencing resistance to the option to stay. The first set of questions tried to shove me into the "right" decision based on exterior perspectives. The second set of questions moved me toward an "authentic" decision based upon my own values and desires.

Learning to approach my thoughts and feelings from a place of curiosity rather than judgment has been an enormous aid for me along my Selah Journey. It allows me to expand into knowledge and truth instead of contracting into defensiveness. It disarms the fear that rises up and meets it with compassion and clarity. It promotes growth, authenticity, and contentment in my present moments. As you embark on your Selah Journey, don't leave without packing your curiosity!

CHAPTER 6

GRATITUDE AND PRAISE

At the beginning of my Selah Journey, I was coming from a place of fear and defeat. My soul had lived in a state of depression for so long that I felt blocked from all that was good. I remembered times in which I recognized glimpses of joy, love, and hope, but I was so thoroughly enveloped by a gray fog that those moments evaporated before they could reach my soul. I even remember feeling angry when others would suggest, "Just focus on what makes you happy," or "Choose to see the positive." It felt impossible. When I did muster up the courage to try, it felt forced and unauthentic.

But then my lifelong friend, Jen, gave me a Gratitude Journal. A blue book with a golden tree on the front. Inside was one page for every day of the year—365 pages of gratitude. Each page provided a space to record the year and just one thing I was grateful for each day. Just one. This was repeated five times so that each page would eventually hold five years of gratitude moments, year after year. She used this journal in her own practices, so in an attempt to meet me where I was, she gifted me one as well.

As thoughtful and kind as the gift was, I carried a healthy portion of skepticism. After all, trying to think happy thoughts hadn't worked for me yet, so why would this be different? Additionally, I self-identify as hopelessly inconsistent when it comes to journaling anything that requires daily attention. My ever-protective ego reminded me this was doomed to failure and to be prepared for my perfectionism to be triggered and my fog of apathy to absorb whatever goodness I was to gain. However, I was desperate to find a way forward, so I accepted the journal, acknowledging the kindness and love Jen had offered with it.

As I began this new practice, I noticed something begin to sprout, so tiny and tender I didn't know if it would survive. Instead of trying to be positive and happy when I simply wasn't, this practice helped me identify just one thing every day that was real and true. This one concrete thing was something for which I could say thank you. It was more than wishful thinking or rose-colored glasses. On the contrary, it connected me with something tangible and concrete. Something I could see as a gift, whether from Spirit, from someone else, or from my own soul. Like little mementos, I collected my expressions of gratitude within the journal and experienced a shifting in my heart.

Recognizing the power contained in this simple practice, I learned that Selah was incomplete if it was simply the twin practices of resting from the demands upon us and reflection on what was true. In order to complete the experience, Selah also required acknowledging that which is good and true in our life, day by day. Living in Gratitude.

*"Gratitude
is the
pathway that
leads from
happiness
to joy."*

NERD NOOK:
GRATITUDE REWIRES YOUR BRAIN FOR THE BETTER

We live in an amazing time of scientific advancements and exploration. After experiencing the power of gratitude, I wanted to know if it was a placebo-type situation or if there was something more going on under the hood of our heads. Turns out, gratitude does a lot for the brain and has an overall positive impact on those humans who tap into this holistic, feel-good practice.

In *The Neuroscience of Gratitude and Effects on the Brain*, an article found on PositivePsychology.com written by Madhuleena Roy Chowdhury, the author cites multiple studies from the twenty-first century on how gratitude works, what happens in the brain when we practice gratitude, and what positive effects and associations gratitude has on people. In my personal experience of recovering from depression, why did a shift to focusing on gratitude help? Turns out, when we focus on our solutions and what we do have, the feel-good neurotransmitters in our brains, serotonin, dopamine, and oxytocin, surge up and we receive a natural dosage of antidepressant. Gratitude literally bathes our brains in happiness!

Another incredible insight this article revealed is

that as we develop habits of gratitude, we actually train our brains to pay more attention to our positive thoughts and feelings. It basically rewires our brain to quiet what is negative and amplify what is good. Our brain loves patterns, shortcuts, and stability, so the more we choose to focus on gratitude, the more the brain starts looking for what brings us more gratitude on a subconscious level.

I highly recommend this article if you want to take a deeper dive into the power of gratitude, especially if you like to explore the science-backed rationale for how and why gratitude works. In the article, you will find a wide scope of the incredible effects of gratitude including the positive connections it has with our brain, moods, anxiety and depression, grief, resilience, stress, social relationships, physical health, and sleep quality.

You Find What You Look For

Author and writer Ranjani Rao, in her book *Rewriting My Happily Ever After*, states, "By writing what I was grateful for, I learned to look for things that made me smile." I completely resonate with this message. As I began to utilize my newly gifted gratitude journal, I began every morning by mentally reviewing the previous day. I would take note of the kindnesses people extended to me and the beauty of creation I witnessed. I would reflect on what made me feel that spark of happiness, no matter how small, and I would choose one to record in my journal. Gradually, instead of waiting for the next morning to review my day, I began taking notice throughout the day of the moments that gave rise to gratitude in my heart. The more I practiced the habit of gratitude, the more I saw occasions of gratitude popping up like wildflowers throughout my day.

Not only does this reflect what is happening neurologically in our brains as we build and reinforce pathways of gratitude, happiness, and joy, but energetically it allows more of what brings us gratitude to show up in our lives. How does this work? Well, remember when we explored that you are simultaneously a physical being and an energetic being, wrapped up as one complete, incredible person? (Check out chapter two if you need a quick refresher.) As our energetic self experiences the energy of our emotions, those energies can be measured by their frequency. David R. Hawkins, well-known spiritual teacher and psychiatrist, utilized a process by which the different frequencies could be measured, and he distilled the information into a table of the levels of human consciousness. Within this scale, which increases exponentially as the energy shifts, he found that the energy of gratitude falls within the same range as the energy of love and joy. That is powerful positive energy extended into the world! Pair this with another reality uncovered in the world of quantum physics (the laws of our energetic being) which shows us that when we focus our attention or consciousness on something, that something is affected by our attention. The theory here extends to suggest that when we focus on something, like gratitude, the attentive energy expressed acts like a magnet, drawing similar energy back to you. Kind of like a feedback loop. So, when we focus our attention and energy on discovering gratitude in our lives, gratitude is drawn to you! This fuels more gratitude, joy, and love, allowing more of the same to be noticed by you.

This works with any energy. Remember when I described the depressive periods in my life? This reality was at work there as well. In those seasons, I was so attuned to what was lacking and missing in my life, my fear, grief, and guilt, that more of that same energy continued to be drawn to me, keeping me in the downward spiral of depression. A good friend once told me that depression only has the power that you give it. While my much younger self did not understand how that worked, I can now see how deeply true those words are. While each person who has wrestled with mental health challenges has a highly unique experience, developing a practice of gratitude can only supportively escalate us more and more through those seasons into acceptance, peace, and love.

Power of Emotion

Emotions are a gift. They are full of power and insight and connections. However, in a world that tends to value rational, objective thought over the subjective and variable experience of feelings, we have been taught to believe our emotions are untrustworthy. Perhaps we have learned to shove down our feelings so that we aren't "too much" or "too dramatic" for others? Maybe we thought that if we ignored our emotions, especially the negative ones, they would go away? As our feelings rise, so do the thoughts and arguments for why we should restrain our emotions to make room for what is sensible.

*Emotions
are a gift.
They are full
of power and
insight and
connections.*

Let's consider some of those objections that like to creep into our thoughts. The incredible power emotion has in our lives is often overlooked. Why? Because they are nonlogical and are undervalued in a rational society. But even some of our most brilliant minds have challenged us to reconsider this false hierarchy. Basically, we can think of emotions as the combination of our bodily energetic responses interpreted through an inner, subconscious lens that identifies that sensation as a positive response (joy, love, peace, etc.) or a negative response (anger, fear, sadness, etc.). The power in the emotion relates to how strongly we feel it, and the frequency or vibration of the emotion is determined by how we identify with it.

Why does this matter? Just as rational thought is the expression of our cognitive brain, emotions are the energetic expression of our heart-brain. Rational thought is connected with the language of logic; emotional expression is connected with the language of intuition. When we learn how to trust both, and allow them to work with one another instead of pitting them against one another, we become more whole and aligned. Albert Einstein described the relationship between rationality and intuition this way: "The intuitive mind is a sacred gift and the rational mind is a faithful servant. We have created a society that honors the servant and has forgotten the gift." In fact, both Einstein and Steve Jobs recognized intuition as foundational to their discoveries and innovations. We will explore intuition more deeply in another chapter, so for now, let's move forward with the understanding that our emotions are connected with the language of intuition.

Because we are both rational and emotional beings, all of our experiences in life are interpreted and understood through both processes of knowing. What is more, it is first through our emotional responses that every experience is evaluated. Every single one. (The Pixar movie *Inside Out* illustrates this process brilliantly.) We vividly remember some of our experiences because our emotional response to them was so strong. One such memory in my life was the first moment I saw my daughter with my own eyes. This moment is firmly cemented in my experience by the strong emotional responses of significance and love I felt when my precious baby girl rested on my belly, outside of my body for the first time. It is this connection of an experience with emotion that leads us into our thoughts, beliefs, and actions; our head, our hearts, and our hands.

Let's explore how this works to understand the powerful and essential role of our emotions using my example of becoming a mother. My experience was that I witnessed my baby born into this world. When my eyes saw her, I first had a flood of emotions—relief, awe, wonder, and instantaneous love and joy. This was the response of my heart. Then, my head became involved with this experience and when coupled with my emotions allowed me to think about what an incredible moment this was in my life. I had felt a new kind of love for this little human. She needed me, and I needed her. All the moments that led to her birth were part of the process of life that we welcomed and anticipated. I was now a mother, and I believed a part of me was born with her, the part of me that would be in eternal connection with her. Because my head helped me understand the significance and weight of my new reality, I started to do things differently. I slept differently, with a part of me always listening for her to alert me if something wasn't right. I did things to protect her. Once, I tripped while carrying her in the car seat. I will never understand how my body contorted and moved in order to ensure I hit the ground first so that she would barely be jostled! The way I acted in the world, the way my "hands" responded to being a mother stemmed from the love I felt and the understanding of my role as the protector of this precious little being. When what I continued to do, out of my "hands," reinforced the feelings of love and joy I had for her, I continued them. When what I did felt out of alignment with my "heart," I either changed the actions of my "hands" or changed the thoughts and beliefs of my "head" until I found congruity. Maybe you have experienced grief instead of joy on the road to motherhood. Or maybe you have not experienced the transformative experience of parenting. Or maybe your experience as a parent comes from unique circumstances. What is incredible is that your experiences, whatever they may be, give rise to the response of your heart (your emotions), which creates an understanding within your head, which gives rise to the actions of your hands. This loop continues to reinforce itself until it is interrupted or altered by a different emotional response.

The power of our emotions is that we cannot embrace transformation without addressing our emotional foundation that initiated our current cycle of head, heart, and hands. If we want change in our lives, doing so by our thoughts and actions alone is incomplete and ineffective. All three aspects of our being work together, but it is our emotional center that is the lynchpin of transformation.

Gratitude, Happiness, and Joy

If our emotions are the gateway for transformation, then gratitude is our foundational step towards happiness and joy. While these three are linked, they are not the same. To understand the nuanced differences, I will lean upon the wisdom of Brother David Steindl-Rast, the Benedictine monk known around the world as the "grandfather of gratitude."

Brother David's Ted Talk from June 2013, "Want to be happy? Be grateful", has been viewed over nine million times on ted.com. It is fifteen minutes of transformational wisdom gifted to us by this humble man. In his talk, he asserts that we all want to be happy. Sounds reasonable. But it is not circumstances that make us happy. Rather, Brother David insists, "It is not happiness that makes us grateful. It's gratefulness that makes us happy." Cultivating an awareness of gratitude gives rise to happiness. And we all have the same ability to recognize gratitude, every moment of every day. "Grateful people are joyful people...grateful people are happy people," David declares. Now, I won't give away all that is in his talk, so you will have to go and watch it for yourself, but we will gratefully (wink, wink) receive his wisdom that gratitude is the key to unlocking happiness and joy.

Happiness and joy are close cousins, but they are a bit different from one another. Happiness arises as a feeling in response to something we experience. A child giggling with glee as he runs through a sprinkler on a hot day makes me feel happy. I can watch ocean waves rhythmically surge over a white sand beach and feel happy. I can feel the gentle rain fall on my face after a long season of drought and feel happy. Happiness is a feeling triggered by our experiences of noticing and recognizing something good in our lives. Joy runs even deeper than happiness. Instead of being a feeling that comes and goes, it is a condition that is cultivated in our lives from a sense of well-being. Many religions link joy with the condition of our spirit when we are at peace and in the right relationship between Spirit and ourselves. Whatever your beliefs, joy taps into the universal and deep truth that at our source, we are whole, and every day we can trust that truth to fuel our being.

Understanding the synergy of our experiences, emotions, and beliefs illuminates why gratitude is so pivotal. It is an actionable emotion that we can utilize by building practices into our life rhythms to identify and embrace more gratitude in our lives. Traveling across the globe has allowed me the privilege of experiencing the varied customs, beliefs, and rhythms embraced by people who are more like me than I ever imagined. As Brother David reminded us, our one commonality is that we all want to be happy. We all have access to the pathway that leads from happiness to joy through the practice of gratitude. In that spirit, when I travel, the first word I strive to learn is how to say "thank you" in the native language of the people. I can think of no better way to acknowledge the truth that I am enriched by the people I encounter. No matter how you say it: Gracias (Spanish), Merci (French), Shukran (Arabic), Asante Sana (Swahili), Matur Suksma (Balinese), or Zikomo Kwambiri (Chichewa) cultivates gratitude.

The
PARTNERS

CHAPTER 7

YOUR SELAH TRIBE

The teenage years are rough for everyone on some level. Puberty. High school. Family dynamics. Identity development. Within it all, each person is trying to figure out who they are and where they fit in within an ocean of opinions, suggestions, criticism, and confusion. Nestled within the ups and downs of the rite of passage called adolescence, one of my teachers, Mr. Woodard, stands out in my memory.

Mr. Woodard was my seventh-grade math teacher, with a head full of curly permed brown hair, a smile on his face, and a song on his lips. Starting junior high brought plenty of firsts: choosing classes, exploring the jungle of hallway lockers, and surviving the daily gym discipline of running around "three fields and the pond." (Shoutout to Paradise Junior High—if you know, you know!) In the midst of all the newness, math was a familiar and easy class for me. That was until Mr. Woodard asked me if I had considered auditioning for his chorus/drama class. It was one of the electives that I hadn't considered because I felt shy. "Come by after school today and you can audition." After school,

I did just that and promptly became one of the chorus/drama kids for the next two years.

After junior high, Mr. Woodard followed our class of students over to the high school. Advanced chorus became a place of welcome on my schedule for the next three years. I learned a lot about myself during that time: I could sing, I could harmonize, being on a stage didn't freak me out, and I loved creating music. It was fun! But one of the biggest lessons I learned (repeatedly) happened when one of us got a haircut.

Whenever someone got a haircut, Mr. Woodard noticed. No matter who you were or what was going on, at the beginning of class he would have you sit down in a single chair in front of everyone, and the entire chorus group would sing "Happy Haircut to you" in the tune of the traditional birthday song. When it was my turn to be singled out, my Irish-toned face would turn a few different shades of red as embarrassment flooded my body. It was an unforgettable experience that we both hated and loved by the time we graduated.

Why did we grow to love being singled out and good-naturedly teased every time we got a haircut? Because each time it happened, we were noticed. We were treated with the same recognition and good-natured teasing as everyone else in the room. We were in the place where we belonged. No one outside that room got this treatment; it was a rite of passage to all who belonged in the group. And it told us every single time that we were seen and celebrated.

Your Travel Partners

Traveling your Selah Journey is an incredibly personal experience. It is also impossible to accomplish this journey without a community. Your Selah Tribe is the community of people you allow to be a part of this journey with you. They are the ones who provide you with what you cannot give yourself; they witness your journey, support your transformation, and remind you that you are seen.

When my physical Selah Journey began, I did not know what I was doing. I had reached my breaking point and something had to change, so I ran away from my current life into the space that had represented home for me from my earliest memories. All I knew was that I needed space to figure out what had happened and what came next. Upon arrival, the first thing I did was begin to draw in a couple of trusted friends because I needed support. I needed someone to know where I was so that if I got in over my head I could reach out for help. I also quickly discovered that in my hasty exit, I left my tent poles back in Colorado! Whoops! So I reached out for help to Brooks and Mauny, two men who had known me for decades. That first night, they showed up with dinner, a tent (with poles!), and unconditional (albeit slightly confused) support on the first night of my transformational journey.

Here's the thing—when I felt the floor of my life drop out from underneath me and I was free falling into the unknown, I didn't want people around me who looked like they had it all together and could swoop in with a solution gift wrapped with a catchy phrase. I wanted people around me who had lived through their own hellish life experiences and could relate to being in a place where survival was goal number one. I wanted people around me who understood that what was about to unfold during the next few weeks was going to be messy and ugly, and they would stand by in the ugly. I wanted people around me who would let me fall apart and would keep me safe and seen while I did the work of putting myself back together.

Over the next few weeks, my Selah Tribe organically grew into a small community that witnessed me and my mess without judgment. They listened to my chaotic and rambling thoughts as I sought to understand how I ended up in this predicament. They offered thoughtful prompts and questions to nudge me toward being honest with myself, even when it scared the shit out of me. This immediate community became my net of safety that watched my back when I was vulnerable, listened to me without trying to fix me, and held a mirror of honest reflection up for me as I sought to remember who I was. These were the ones who I allowed into my journey, and I am the better for it.

Looking back, I can see some of the essential qualities the individuals in my tribe had in common.

Trust. I completely trusted each person who became part of my tribe. Trust is earned, and this group of individuals had enough history with me that I knew I could trust them. Over the thirty years of my knowing each one of them, we had shared stories, shown up, and valued one another. Each person was someone I felt safe with. In those early days, I was incredibly vulnerable and not entirely myself. With these people at the ready, I knew I could lean into our friendships and that they would let me be a mess, but not so much of a mess that I would act on my stupid inclinations. I could trust them with my words, with my actions, and with my making-it-up-as-I-went process.

Different experiences and backgrounds. The variety of personalities and life experiences represented in my Selah Tribe was an incredible blessing. This diversity allowed them to share the weight of support I required among the group. Different individuals provided different kinds of support. Some of them directly called me out when I needed to hear hard truths. Some would listen as I verbally processed my thoughts and emotions. Some of them reminded me of the progress I was making and cheered me on as I stayed the course. Others were a sounding board, allowing me to hear my own thoughts from different perspectives. Some of them assured me I wasn't crazy when I felt certain I was. Some provided meals and beds when the weather would shift and I needed a bit more than a tent and camp stove. Having a tribe meant I had multiple avenues of support, protection, and kindness.

Love without expectations. Each one of these friends had known me for at least thirty years. In that time, we had allowed one another to come in and out of each other's lives as circumstances allowed. We knew the character of one another and had witnessed what remained constant in each other throughout life's changes and challenges. Each member of my tribe cared about me enough to hold me in love throughout this time of crisis and transformation. At the same time, each member of my tribe only wanted what was best for me, regardless of what that looked like for others. They loved me without feeling expected to fix me.

Having a tribe meant I had multiple avenues of support, protection, and kindness.

As you embark on your own Selah Journey, it is good to be selective about whom you allow into your Selah Tribe. This is your pathway, your goals, your process, your transformation. It is not a time to let people in because they might feel hurt being left out of your process. I felt that way about my family. I love them to pieces! In fact, it was my love for them that drove me to care for them so much that I sacrificed my own well-being. They didn't ask me to; I chose it. Had I invited them in, my Selah Journey would have been hindered by my people-pleasing nature that had taken over my life. I have no doubt they would have supported me and loved me completely. That is who they are. However, I had lost my own identity by allowing them to define who I was supposed to be and how I was supposed to show up in the world. I lost myself as I desired to be the person I thought they wanted me to be. My Selah Journey was about rediscovering and learning to accept and love who I am authentically at my core. I had to recover that version of myself. In order to do so I needed a tribe that provided me the freedom to explore without feeling obligated to please them. My journey was about me. Your journey is about you. Your travel companions have to afford you the freedom to do just that—explore who you are at your core.

My tribe continues to grow as I still follow my Selah Journey pathway. This initial group walked with me intently for the first year as I was in a steep learning curve about my life, my choices, and my sense of self. They served an incredibly special purpose in my life and for that, I am forever grateful. The truth is, while our individual Selah Journeys are intensely personal, they are not meant to be solo trips. As you consider whom you will allow to witness your process and transformation, make sure: you trust them, respect and value their unique perspective, and that they want to see you thrive for your sake.

People You Meet Along the Way

When traveling it is the people who make the journey unforgettable. Some of those people are the ones on the trip with you, and others are those you meet along the journey. I remember for one of my cross-country trips, I planned my entire route around the people I wanted to connect with! Not the most efficient route, but by far one of my most memorable and fulfilling trips. Along the journey, I also tend to meet the most interesting people! Recently, on a trip through New England, my husband joined me at breakfast as I was getting to know a delightful couple from Texas. They were wrapping up a family trip after visiting five New England states in six days with their kids. Listening to the mother of that beautiful family took me back to when I started road-tripping with my kids and the wonder of exploring states that used to be just colored blocks on a map.

Along your Selah Journey, as you explore your pathway of rest, reflection, and gratitude, you will discover people who will cross your path for such a time as this. I like to think of these as sacred appointments with those we get to learn from on our transformative journey. One such person for me was April Adams Pertuis. I was just becoming acquainted with April at the beginning of my first Selah Journey. She and another mentor of mine, Alexandra Taketa, had invited me into a small circle of women designed to equip me to explore my passion and turn it into my purpose. These women, and my fellow cohort members, provided a structured time for me to attempt to believe and find the good in what I was experiencing. Had I known I would have a full-blown life crisis in the midst of our program, I would never have said yes! But Spirit knew what I needed and provided it before I had a clue as to how essential it would be to my process.

Since that summer in 2021, April has become a mentor, a teacher, a guide, and a treasured friend to me. She has taught me how to unpack my story and grow into the necessary confidence and skills needed to share through her storytelling formula. She never lets me forget how important my story is and continues to provide opportunities and connections for me to build upon so that I can shine as a light for those who will embrace The Selah Journey. She is one of my people, a member of my tribe, who I met along the way. She has empowered me with her knowledge, persistence, and passion at just the right time, in just the right way.

Remember when we talked about how our energy attracts similar energy? When we start exercising restorative rest, reflective curiosity, and gratitude practices, others who are engaging with that same energy will be drawn to you, and you to them. Another way to look at this is that as we learn, grow, and transform in our lives, Spirit sends us the right people to help us at the right time. These are divine connections, beautiful souls sent to help us along our journey. These are the teachers and guides appointed to us to support our transformation and help us grow into our whole, authentic selves.

May I ask you a question? What prompted you to pick up this book? What were you hoping to gain from your time spent exploring the pages? However you came to this book, I believe it has something to offer you. As I reflect on my experiences, you might glean some insight from its pages. There is something

*As we learn,
grow, and
transform in our
lives, Spirit sends
us the right people
to help us at
the right time.*

here for you; information, support, perspective or inspiration, or a camaraderie. Just as your energy attracted this book to you, I am writing this book with the energy of intention that anyone who could use a compassionate and honest voice on their road to freedom will find just that, right here. The energy of love, empathy, and hope that I am pouring into this book has made its way into your hands and is meant for you, and maybe even for someone you know.

Those who intersect with you at key moments along your trek are there to serve as guides, mentors, and teachers. Just as April was (and still is) for me, Spirit has appointed individuals along your pathway to teach you, guide you, and cheer you on. Since your journey is highly personal to you, I can't tell you who they are, but I suggest some ways you might spot them. First, travel your Selah Journey with openness and awareness. You will need some help from others along the way, so pay attention to the people you meet. Is there something about them that pulls you towards them? Do you resonate with them in some way? Are you encountering people who represent a common theme with you? Be open to the real opportunities to learn from others who are all around you. You have a responsibility to yourself to pay attention and notice what is coming your way. Also, look for what flows and feels good. In the world of spirit and energy, connections are not forced; they are received. Sacred timing is a very real thing. If you are trying to make a connection with someone, and it just isn't working, let it go. Likely it isn't the right timing. Look for who and what is flowing towards you and be curious about where you feel connection. As you meet people along your path, keep your eyes open and pay attention. Help is all around you and will be there when you are ready.

NERD NOOK:
MASLOW HAS A SOCIAL POINT

SELF-ACTUALIZATION NEEDS

SELF-ESTEEM NEEDS

LOVE AND BELONGING NEEDS

SAFETY NEEDS

PHYSIOLOGICAL NEEDS

Abraham Maslow was an American psychologist who is widely known for his Hierarchy of Needs. His model outlines five stages of needs common to all humans. It also illustrates how each level of needs provides the foundation the next group of needs is built upon. For example, in Maslow's hierarchy, the Physiological needs of food, water, shelter, clothing, etc., are the most basic. Without access to or confidence in this first group of needs, the next group of Security needs has no strong foundation to be built upon.

If you look at the triangle, social needs are layered all throughout the triangle beyond the base. At the Safety and Security stage, we look for a sense of family and social connections. At the Love and Belonging stage, we seek intimacy, friendship, and connection. The Self-Esteem stage seeks the respect of others, and the Self-Actualization stage desires a moral base, and purpose, which involves how we understand our role in the global community. Humans are social creatures, and Maslow's Hierarchy illustrates just how foundational social engagement is to our development.

To illustrate this point, consider why solitary confinement is used in prisons. This punitive practice is designed to take away a person's basic human need for social interaction. As a result, various studies have documented links between solitary confinement and anxiety, depression, paranoia, increased drug use, sleep disturbances, memory impairment, decreased brain functioning, weakened cardiovascular system, and increased suicide attempts and completions. As a punishment, the consequences of social isolation are so severe that there is a movement to end the practice as it does little for rehabilitation and instead, does significant harm mentally, physically, and socially to the individual. While this is an extreme illustration, it does highlight the necessary and fundamental role of social engagement and interaction in our lives.

Contrast that with the benefits that come with connections in community. A quick survey of behavioral health and wellness articles highlights multiple benefits of community including: support, safety, connection, a sense of belonging, positive influence, learning, positive emotions, greater success, positive shifts in self-worth, stress reduction, lower blood pressure, and lower cholesterol. Comparing what results from community connections, or the lack thereof, it becomes obvious that the pathway to holistic health and well-being must involve community and social influences.

Community Is Key

For as far back as history records, we see humans living with one another in family groups and communities. Severe punishments within these communities involve being isolated from your community, like being imprisoned, or even being exiled from your community, forced into the outside world to find your way alone. Why? Life is harder and more dangerous alone. Communities provide protection and partnerships that enrich our lives and lighten the load of daily living. Together we are stronger than we are apart. More than that, together we better know and understand ourselves.

In college, our school hosted an outdoor adventure program called La Vida. Participating in one of the offered outdoor programs was a graduation requirement, so I signed up for the two-week summer hiking trip in May with a collection of seven other students, all seeking to check this box off their list. The seven of us spent our time together traversing the Adirondack Mountains of New York under the leadership of three peers while learning all kinds of outdoorsy skills. Even more importantly, we were learning more about ourselves and how to work with others.

At the end of our experience, we shared our H.A.C.s with one another: our Hopes, Affirmations, and Challenges. Before our final evening together, each one of us spent time considering the others on our trip. Based on our experiences and conversations with one another, we recorded a hope, an affirmation, and a challenge for each person on our team. Then, one by one, we took turns being the center of attention and receiving these gifts shared with us from each member of our team.

It was humbling to be the center of attention in this way. It was also an early lesson for me in how to receive kind words alongside constructive critique. What is more, after just two weeks of sharing life together, I recognized that they, as my community, saw things within me that I was unaware of or inattentive to. From their varied perspectives, they gifted to me a hope for my future, an affirmation of my being, and a challenge for growth.

Together, we better know and understand ourselves. Together, we are seen, and allow others to be seen. Together, we strengthen and build up one another.

Transformation is incomplete when done alone. Without the perspectives and insights spoken in love and truth from others, we cannot discover what is in our blind spots. But isn't it beautiful that when we don't know what we don't know, your Selah tribe can be there to give you the insight that only they have?

CHAPTER 8

YOUR BEST AND HIGHEST SELF

On the left-hand side of my computer, in the lower corner, I have a faded pink sticky note that reads, "Today and Everyday, I Am My Higher Self." I see it every time I sit at my computer to write a story or meet with a coaching client. It is an ordinary and everyday reminder that all of who I am, my past and potentially perfected future, already exists. And she is available to me at all times.

The first time someone introduced this idea to me, I was skeptical. How can this be real? Does my faith and religious belief have room for this? How can I be sure? This can't be true... it's all subjective and in my head, right? Doubt and dis-ease came rushing forward, trying to protect me in case it was too good to be true and I experienced hurt or disappointment. But then, I met her... I mean me.

Heather Alice Shea was leading our class of intuitive coaching students when she walked us through the most beautifully guided meditation. I remember envisioning walking through a field, with a stream running alongside me. I crossed over a wooden bridge and walked barefoot towards the forest that edged the meadow. In front of me, my best and highest self walked through the doorway of a humble cabin, with arms outstretched, welcoming me home. She radiated with a strong yet gentle confidence. There was no doubt within her about who she was in the world. She carried herself with purpose and patience flowing from her beach-wavy hair to her loose natural clothing. Neither rushed nor idle, she held my hand, and I felt overwhelming compassion and love. She was me in full freedom being exactly who I am designed to be.

She is all of the potential of me embodied for my highest good, and the highest good of those in my community, and the world. And she is with me always, walking with me as I walk into my future.

I met my highest self almost two years ago. Since then, I am always aware of our connection, and I feel her presence with me. She is a comfort and a guide to me. Knowing me fully, seeing me truly, and reminding me of the promise that is unfolding in my life, she is a constant companion for me along my Selah Journey.

Just imagine, one of your truest travel companions along your Selah Journey is your Best and Highest Self. They are with you, whether you realize it or not. They are for you, no matter what circumstances you may be facing. They want what is good and best for you, continually reminding you of who you know you really are. They are here for the journey with you, so lean into all your best self has for you along the way.

Let's Back Up—Who Is Your Highest Self?

Remember back in chapter three when we discussed how we are simultaneously physical and energetic in our being? We are constructed of both atoms (our physical being) and photons (our energetic being). The scientific genius of Albert Einstein introduced us to the concept that energy cannot be created or destroyed. It can be transmuted or changed, but it always exists. Without going too far down this rabbit hole (that would require a different book), the energy of who you are always exists. It exists in the past, the present, and the future all at the same time. As this photon-based energetic being, you exist outside the bounds of time and space. And although quantum physics is just beginning to understand how and why all this works, the fact of the matter for us is that you exist energetically, always. This allows for the energetic you of right now to connect with the you that is fully actualized in all his or her potential. The you that you can become and are becoming. The youiest you you can be. This You is your best and highest self.

When we lean into our intuition and acknowledge all that we are in this world, we connect with our inner wisdom, the highest you, and can receive all their guidance, counsel, and perspective. How incredibly awesome is that! You are one of your best travel companions along your Selah Journey, because who knows you better than you—in all of your past, present, and future potential!

But Cami, how can I trust this? How is this different than wishful thinking? I hear you, my friend. Just like any relationship, trust is built over time and with every encounter you have with one another. This is a relationship of building trust with yourself. To gain a little perspective, let's look at it from a different angle.

Think back to your childhood. Each of us has a unique experience. No matter how happy or challenging, how abundant or lacking our childhood was, it was imperfect. When imperfect people come together, an imperfect family is created. And no matter what the intentions are, no one person can understand and meet perfectly the needs of a child. We are all in-process! When I was a child, my parents were still becoming who they were meant to be. They were incredible in the areas they had developed a maturity in throughout their lives. However, there were some skills and qualities that were still developing. You cannot give what you do not have and have not yet learned. And I say this in the deepest of love because I experienced this humbling reality when I became a parent. Becoming a parent is an on-the-job learning process. No amount of preparation is adequate for the moment when another beautifully unique individual is dependent upon you for absolutely everything.

In that child, a wealth of potential exists. In you, as an infant, a wealth of potential was born. That potential was able to grow and develop in the areas where you were nurtured and given the freedom to expand. However, other areas experienced a lack, because no one grows up in a perfect family. In my childhood, for example, I was given the gift of education, which allowed me to experience my academic potential. However, I developed a lack in my own self-esteem because my experiences led me to believe I was loved for my accomplishments, not my being. This part of my personal development matured more slowly than other parts of who I am. As I continued to be praised for my performances, my understanding that my value lay within what I produced continued to be reinforced. I continued on that limited path until I could no longer ignore the pain it produced in my life.

When I look back on that part of me, I have deep compassion and love. Why? Because I was doing the best I could with what I had been given. My parents did not know how to give praise to their children in the way I needed, because they needed or received praise differently from their own parents. They could not give what they did not understand. Their intentions towards me and love for me were good, just imperfect as we all are imperfect. If I could go back, I would shower my younger self with affirmations that who she is was good enough. I would remind her that her value is inherent because she reflects and represents her Creator. I would challenge her that who she is, is worth far more than what she does.

Now that I have found healing in understanding who I am, as the higher/future version of that little girl, I can thank her for her perseverance and patience. This is the magic of this relationship. The me that is here now was always with that little girl. And that little girl is always a part of who I am now. The potential carried by my younger self is more clearly actualized in who I am today. In the same way, the potential I still carry with me now is actualized in my higher self, the self I am becoming. She is with me now and always, the same way the present me was with my younger self. As a little girl, I did not know how to connect with the future me. But now, I do. And that future, higher me can guide and lead me into what is still to come.

As we continue this exploration, I want to make a crucial note. It is also true that as we have potential for great good (our

"Today and everyday, I am my Higher Self."

higher self), we also have potential for great evil (our lower self). That potential exists as well, and we do ourselves a disservice by ignoring this truth. Religions around the world acknowledge this reality: we possess incredible capacity towards both our highest potential as well as our most base nature. This idea is mirrored in quantum physics that suggests every potential version of ourselves is possible and exists. Where we set our attention is where we will go. When we continually focus on all our desperation and lack, we will move in that direction. But when we attend all the ways we are growing and thriving, we move ourselves along that more powerful pathway. Let us not forget the importance our intentions bring into who we are becoming.

NERD NOOK:
ENERGETIC HYGIENE

As we expand our understanding of our energetic self, it is important to recognize that the practice of energetic hygiene is just as important as practicing physical hygiene. As we go through our day, we connect with others all the time, sometimes without realizing it. As an empath, I experience this all the time. Others can "sense" that I can connect with them on an emotional level and therefore seek out my presence, and my listening ear, as they tell me about their lives, challenges, hurts, and joys. And as an empath, before I understood about my energetic self, I would reach the end of my day feeling drained or sad—not because I was feeling those emotions, but because others had shared their emotional stories with me and I didn't know how to disconnect. Energetic hygiene is a practice where we regularly clean up and strengthen our energetic field, much like we can wash our hands, brush our teeth, and eat nutritious foods to keep our physical self healthy.

As we discussed in chapter three, use your imagination to visualize your toroidal field as an energetic egg that extends off your body and surrounds it. This energy field is you, radiating from your heart's neural pathways and connecting you with your intuitive pathways. You are sovereign in this space. You set and control your boundaries here. You have a say over what can enter your energy and what can stay connected to your energy.

Now, is there someone that keeps coming to mind? If so, they are likely connected to your energy. Either they are reaching out to you energetically, or you have connected with them somehow and have allowed the connection to remain. Picture or feel that connection in your field. See it? Feel it? When you are ready to let it go, imagine a sword or a blade cutting that connection and sending it back to that person in love.

Another technique I use, called the "feather duster," is a general cleaning up of my toroidal field to keep it clear and receptive. I will envision the toroidal field surrounding me and holding me. And then, in my mind, I pull out a feather duster and wave it all around, with the intention of catching anything that no longer serves me well, sending it dancing and flying back into the universe.

Although there is some playfulness and imagination flowing in these examples, they are powerful ways to engage your sovereignty over yourself. Imagine if we continually connected with people without discretion, allowing dysfunction and the intentions of others to have influence over us all the time. Just as tiny germs and viruses can slow down and damage our physical bodies, so can ill intentions or the lower energies of anger, shame, and guilt slow down and hinder our energetic bodies. Being clear with your intentions and boundaries and doing some regular cleaning up within your energetic field are important hygienic practices so you can be the best possible You.

Building Your Connection with You

So how can you regularly engage with your highest self and nurture the connection between her and your current, embodied self?

Let's start by remembering your highest self is with you at all times. They are part of your being, and you are never without them. Connecting with them can be as simple as remembering their presence is with you always. However, it is also true that as human beings, rhythms and personal rituals are powerful tools that help us remember and connect with what is in the unseen world.

My first intentional encounter with my best self was facilitated through a guided visualization. With the aid of someone else's voice and direction, I walked through a few steps: setting my intentions, getting into my present moment, allowing my attention to shift from my physical world into my inner world, and utilizing the tool of imagination to help me experience the connection with my best self. Using this as a guide, you can build your own ritual to connect.

To begin, set your intention. Prepare your physical and energetic self for what this ritual is intended to accomplish. Say to yourself, "I am ready to meet and connect with my highest and best self. I only intend on connecting with my highest and best self. The me that is for my highest good and the highest good of my community and the world." You can use these words or others depending on what feels right for you. The point is to be clear with your intention. Set that intention in whatever way feels most organic for you.

Next, get present in the moment of "now." Our thoughts can fluctuate between our current reality, our past experiences, and our future plans like that little metal ball in a pinball machine. So, take a few moments or breaths to get present. Maybe you light a candle and focus on the flame. Maybe you take some deep focused breaths, experiencing the air as it enters your lungs and exhales what you no longer need. Maybe you close your eyes and take note of what you hear, feel, smell, or taste. Maybe you mentally scan your body and notice what it is experiencing in the moment. Whatever process best helps you to get present in your now…practice that.

Next, allow your attention to shift from your physical-now into your inner world. Typically, people tend to close their eyes at this point, but if you want to keep them open, hold a soft gaze at a spot out in front of you. In your mind, you could walk through a mental image of being in a space where you are comfortable, like a sunny spring meadow at the foot of a hill, on the shore of a peaceful lake, or on a pathway leading you toward a forest. (I like nature imagery, can you tell?) You can create your own place in your mind's eye that allows you to just be you, comfortably. If imagery is not your thing, focus on your heart space, and begin to notice what your emotions, will, and desires are sharing with you. Listen or feel what comes up for you as you shift your attention inward to your soul. Whatever your process, allow your focus to move from your physical-now into your inner-now.

Finally, shift through your mental space upward, either up a pathway, a hill, or even a staircase, but move your attention upward. As you move upward, cross a threshold of some sort: a bridge, a doorway, over the crest of a hill or path. When you cross that threshold, notice who is coming toward you. You have crossed over into the space of your higher self, and they are there ready for your arrival. When they appear, notice what they look like. How does it feel to be in their presence? Take some time to experience the connection. Again, if visualizing doesn't come naturally to you, then move your awareness from your inner mind or heart upward and outward from your being just a bit. Pay

*All practices
within your
Selah Journey
must be
aligned and
authentic with
who you are.*

attention to a presence that is ready to receive you and what you experience as you become aware of them.

When you are ready to come back into your physical space, just follow the same steps in reverse. The visualization or ritual helps you get in touch with what is already true about you. This is only one suggestion out of many possibilities to create your pathway of awareness with your best self. As you continue to build your awareness, you may develop a few techniques to shift your focus quickly. Other times you may linger and savor the time within that connection intentionally. Visualizations, breath work, mindfulness, and focal triggers are all possibilities for you to play with as you develop your awareness. Have fun with it!

A word of transparency. Initially, I struggled a bit to understand if my faith tradition allowed for this type of interaction. This was something I took time to pray about and reflect upon in my learning practice. Ultimately, I came to peace with the process, understanding that Spirit already is well acquainted with my highest, best self. She is the potential already given to me by Creator. There is nothing hidden between my highest self and Spirit, so there need not be anything hidden in my connection with God and with my best self. There is freedom for me in connecting with the perfected version of me that Creator knows intimately already. Whatever your faith practice is, spend time in attentive reflection and consideration. All practices within your Selah Journey must be aligned and authentic with who you are. Do not shy away if there is some tension as you learn and experience a new way of knowing yourself. Lean into it and learn. And then move forward in a way that feels aligned and authentic for you.

The Power of Working with Your Highest Self

Working with your Best and Highest Self is a gift. This relationship opens doors of understanding, compassion, wisdom, direction, and power. Who knows your potential better than your own self? Who desires what is best for you in life and relationships? Your highest self has only you as their focus and desire. They want what is best for you, what is aligned for you, what is expansive and enriching for you. When I first started learning about intuition, Heather Alice Shea taught me the root definition of the word intuition: "to contemplate upon the teaching from your inner watcher or guard." Your inner watcher or guard is your highest self.

These things are also true for your Creator, which we will look at in the next chapter. For now, understand that through the connection with your highest self, you readily receive knowledge and insight in a way that is uniquely personal to you. With access to all you have been in your past, and all you are capable of in the future, you are provided with information, encouragement, challenge, and understanding tailored to who you are in the present. Imagine standing in relationship with one who truly sees how you have struggled and endured; how you have fallen short and disappointed yourself; how you have overcome and accomplished personal victories. And then you see them beaming with pride and compassion, reminding you of how incredible you are, and are becoming. One who is like your true friend, celebrating your successes, marking your milestones, and admonishing you to stay true to who you are all along the journey.

Another incredible strength of reinforcing the connection with your higher self is that your energy can flow powerfully between you and yourself. Consider the fact that as we go through our day, we engage with other people and their energy all the time. Within our homes, we are physically within one another's energetic fields throughout the day. We encounter friends and strangers when we go out to shop or run errands, encountering more energetic fields. We can chat on the phone and connect with family and loved ones from a distance—energetically we connect. And then there are those people who live in our heads, rent-free, as we recall past hurts and relational wounds that we still carry with us. There are so many ways in which we connect with others energetically. This can leave us feeling drained and scattered at times as if we have strings tugging us in different directions.

So, when it comes to our purpose, decisions, and direction, it helps to have our energy aligned and clear. When we are energetically connected to our highest and best self we create a strong closed loop. When it comes to the care and keeping of you, ultimately, you are sovereign over yourself. You have agency and choice to make decisions about who you are becoming and how you want to conduct yourself. You have the authority to decide what to pursue in life and what to let go of. You are the CEO of you. While it can be good to seek counsel and perspective from others, when it comes to your decisions and choices, only you have the sovereignty to determine the path of your character and person. Who better to consult with than you? You are the one who fully lives with your decisions, so you are also the one who fully makes those decisions for yourself and all that affects your life.

If you are a person of faith, as I am, much of this perspective also applies to your personal relationship with Spirit/

Creator. However, like any relationship, our engagement with our Spiritual Source can be complicated at times. Like our highest self, most faith traditions affirm that Spirit desires what is best for us as humanity, personally and collectively. But what happens when we struggle with trusting Creator's goodness when we are walking through a tragic loss in our life, or are feeling distant and disconnected from Spirit? My personal history with chronic depressive disorder reminds me that sometimes Creator feels impossible to access. In those times, I sometimes find it easier to connect with my higher self, who is also fully known and seen by Creator and wants all the goodness for me that Spirit desires. I'm not suggesting we intentionally disconnect from Creator but instead recognize what a blessing it is that we can always trust our best self to have our best intentions at heart, even when we may be working through a point of struggle with Spirit.

CHAPTER 9

YOUR SPIRITUAL SOURCE

Do you remember your teenage years? That awkward time between childhood and adulthood. Old enough to be responsible for yourself, but immature enough to make a mess of things along the way. I remember those years of feeling smart and afraid and confused and insecure and unstoppable almost all at the same time. It was during that time in my life that I began to take more personal responsibility over my faith. I knew what had been taught to me by family and friends, but I was exploring how trustworthy those teachings really were. How could I be sure of the beliefs I had learned?

During these same teenage years, I attended a religious camp one summer with my lifelong friend, Casey. At the end of the week, we were presented with the opportunity to make a personal choice about what we believed. Did I want to personally commit to following Creator? I remember asking Spirit to be part of my life when I was a child, but I was older now. This wasn't about passively accepting what I had been taught as I grew up. This was about actively taking responsibility for the beliefs and actions I would choose and follow. Did I trust the stories about Creator that I had been told by my mom? Did I believe what I had read in the Hebrew Scriptures and the Christian New Testament? If this Spirit was real, what would it look like for me to be a follower? Would this Creator accept me? Love me? Help me? Guide me? Could I trust Them?

I remember having an honest talk with Spirit as I wandered outside under the stars that evening. I was praying, expressing to my Creator that I did believe S/He was who the Holy Scriptures said S/He was, but I didn't understand what it would be like to be in a relationship with the Creator of all. I knew how to connect with other people through conversation, time spent together, and affection, but what did that look like with a Spirit I could not touch or hear? As I continued to pray, it started to feel like I was talking to the air, without response. I felt that I shouldn't want or ask for some sort of confirmation that S/He was listening to me. After all, I was just a teenager, no one special. But wouldn't it be nice to have some sort of sign that helped me learn how to trust in Spirit's presence? I didn't need a sign to believe, just as I didn't feel that I deserved to expect a response. It would just be nice to know S/He was listening.

At that moment, I looked up and watched two shooting stars cross paths with one another in the sky, creating the image of a cross. In the Christian tradition, the cross is a symbol of the perfect love of the Creator. A symbol that reminded me that Spirit took my punishment and consequences for all of the wickedness and wrong I would do in my life, and in exchange for my trust and love, I would be included and secure in Creator's family for all eternity. Seeing this once-in-a-lifetime sight became that assurance I had hesitated to ask for. But my Creator heard me, knew me, and gave me what I needed in that moment.

I take great comfort in knowing that my Spiritual Source, my Creator, is listening. He is along for my journey, and I have access to Spirit's wisdom and care for me all along the way. No matter your faith tradition, Your Creator knows you and has a purpose for you. I believe that with my whole being. When you embark on your Selah Journey, Spirit is your most powerful guide and ally to have along the way.

Religion and Relationship

That powerful night, the religion I experienced as a child shifted from something I knew about into a relationship between myself and Spirit. And what an incredible ride it has been! I've had moments of delight and confidence, and I've endured seasons of anger and disappointment with my Creator. Being in a relationship with One who is so completely different and eternal and above me is frequently challenging. It is also highly personal. Sometimes one of the biggest challenges within our relationship is the practice of the religion that is supposed to help support my faith in Spirit.

Religious practices and gatherings ideally help educate the follower on what is true and how best to honor the Spirit we follow. I once had a theology instructor, Dr. Peter Anders, who in our first class drew this diagram:

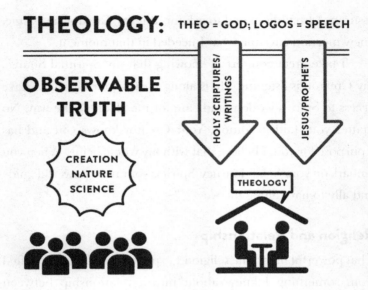

THEOLOGY: THEO = GOD; LOGOS = SPEECH

OBSERVABLE TRUTH

HOLY SCRIPTURES/WRITINGS

JESUS/PROPHETS

CREATION NATURE SCIENCE

THEOLOGY

In the diagram, Creator/Spirit is above the double line that we cannot cross. What Spirit says about Him/Herself is Theology. (Theo = God; Logos = word/speech.) It is the perfect Truth of what Creator expresses about Him/Herself. Below the double line, we are dependent on inferring what is true about Spirit. We do so by observing creation, receiving guidance from our consciousness, and following sacred texts believed to be gifted to us by Creator. Our task as humans is to get our imperfect understanding of theology to best match Spirit's perfect Theology. It is an imperfect task because we are imperfect people. But that doesn't let us off the hook of making an authentic attempt at it.

And here is where religion and relationship with God can get complicated. Not everyone believes the same things, even within the same religion. We are all also at different points along our journey of spiritual maturity. Some of my deepest wounds

Be honest
with yourself
about what
you believe
is true.

and sharpest experiences of injustice have come from people within my faith community. From using my illness as evidence of a lack of faith to falling back on prayer as an excuse to gossip and justify opinions, I have experienced rejection and betrayal. I have also witnessed others feel judged and rejected in religious settings because they don't live up to a particular standard. This same rejection and suspicion is what many people encounter in religious organizations. Why? In religion, we are imperfect people trying to live up to imperfect standards and being judged by more imperfect people working within imperfect practices. All because we have an innate desire to be accepted by and connected with a Creator who holds perfectly our meaning and purpose in life.

It is a tension that has existed for millennia and has been the source of challenges ranging from personal strife to global genocide. I'm not suggesting that I have any answers for this tension on a world stage, but I do affirm that getting real and honest with yourself about who and what you trust and believe is a foundational step for each one of us.

Whether your religion is Science or Christianity, Islam or Atheism, or one of the thousands of recognized religions in the world, I'm asking you to be honest with yourself about what you believe to be true. It is okay to be unsure, or to be in process and still figuring it out. Honestly, we all are! But just as two stars crossing themselves one night in the 1980s confirmed for me there is a Spirit who sees, hears, and answers me, what do you trust and believe as true in your soul? What is your relationship with Spirit? Universe? Creator?

Alignment Brings You Strength

Out of all of your travel partners along The Selah Journey, your Spiritual Source is foundational to your experience. The religious tradition you practice will inform your view of the world as well as your place in this world. Your relationship with Creator is paramount. It is the framework from which everything else derives its shape and structure.

Think of it like your spine, or backbone. If you have ever been under the care of a chiropractor, then you know that one of the first things they do is get an X-ray of your spine. Why? Because the spine is foundational to your health. The support, balance, and communication provided by your spine to the rest of your body are critical. And when your spine is out of alignment, you experience pain. It is the chiropractor's job to help your body become realigned, not just to eliminate your pain, but to allow your whole body optimal use of all of its processes and functions.

Our beliefs stack up, one on top of another, just like our backbone. All of our actions in life come forth from these core beliefs. When our beliefs are weakened, misaligned, or are no longer functioning with who we are becoming, we need to reexamine them to learn what is not working anymore. To illustrate, remember the long-held belief I had that I was to be perfect in all I did? This belief was reinforced in my family and integrated within my faith through my interpretation of their actions and words. So I continued along this path of perfection, adapting to the smaller pain points of feeling accepted only for my actions and feeling as if I was a failure for any small imperfection. It worked (prompting me into excellence) until it didn't anymore (because perfection is impossible in all areas of

*Our beliefs
stack up,
one on top
of another,
just like
our backbone.*

life). At this point, I needed to explore where this belief came from and if it was actually true. In my childhood mind, it was absolutely true! But from a more mature adult understanding, I could see it was misaligned with some other beliefs I held, and they needed to be adjusted.

So how do we engage with Spirit to move into alignment with our purpose and our engagement in the world? That, my friend, is the combination of the knowledge we understand with our heads, the actions we do to honor what we believe, and the intuition we receive through our hearts.

Intuition - The Language of Spirit

In order to work with Spirit, we need to understand how to hear what Spirit communicates with us. This is where intuition comes in! Whether you realize it or not, you are intuitive. You are equipped and designed to receive information from your Spiritual Source through the language of intuition. You are intuitive. 100%. That time you just knew something to be true, but didn't know why you knew it, that was your intuition. That time you felt overwhelmingly emotional because someone you are close with was grieving, that was your intuition. That whisper of your conscience that admonished you to do what you knew to be right—that was your intuition. That song that was stuck on repeat in your head and you didn't know why—that was your intuition. Unbeknownst to you, your intuitive senses picked up on energetic signals and gave you directions and feelings to act in a way that was beyond your understanding.

Just as you have the five physical senses that allow you to see, hear, smell, touch, and taste what is happening in the physical world, you also have eight energetic senses that allow you to take in information from the energetic world. Sometimes we call these senses our "sixth sense" or our "spidey-sense." More accurately, they are known as "clairs," which means clear in French. These eight senses are:

- ⊚   Clairvoyance = clear seeing: images you see in your mind
- ⊚   Clairaudience = clear hearing: that voice and sound you hear within your mind
- ⊚   Claircognizance = clear knowing: being aware of knowledge without knowing how you know
- ⊚   Clairsentience: empathic = clear feeling of emotional energy: feeling the emotions of the room or others as your own
- ⊚   Clairsentience: somatic = clear feeling of physiological sensations: feeling information as a physical sensation in your body
- ⊚   Clairgustance = clear tasting: experiences energetic information by tasting it
- ⊚   Clairsalience = clear smelling: experiencing energetic information as a whiff of a scent
- ⊚   Claritangency = clear touching: receiving information through the touching of objects

It is through our clair senses that we receive energetic information. You are continually taking in information through these gateways. So why don't we recognize the information we receive in this way? Because we have forgotten how to notice it and have diminished our trust in it. This is a nonlinear, nonrational system of information, different from, but not inferior to our rational, logical mind.

This system is how things of Spirit, or things beyond our physical world, can communicate with us. Let me be clear, intuition is not spirituality—instead, it is the vehicle through which spiritual beings communicate with us. This is how you receive information from the Universe, get direction from your conscience, understand truth from Creator, and deeply connect with your friends without words. You are already intuiting without realizing it. What might you learn if you attuned your ability to notice the information you are already receiving?

The prayers, intentions, and rituals we practice through religion help us do just that. They draw our attention inward and upward, focusing beyond our physical surroundings toward what is eternal and expansive. When you light a candle in memory of a family member or a friend, your attention remembers them and you may experience the continued connection you have with that person or hear a word of encouragement or wisdom from their eternal energy. When you walk a path of meditation or prayer, you open more intently to the wisdom Spirit has for you. When you celebrate the anniversary of key moments in your faith tradition, you attune yourself to the energetic vibration and power within those pivotal, key moments.

Just because these experiences and sources of information are subjective does not mean they are untrue. Nonrational, subjective information is not irrational. It is of the world of concept, art, perception, and patterns. And what is Spirit, if not true? We long to make sense of the world and our place in it. For some, science provides a sufficient answer to their questions and they connect with the power of life as understood through the truth of science. For others, religion provides true answers, and the patterns and rituals therein help us connect with the Source of Life. For each of us, the understanding is personal. And just as Dr. Anders illustrated, it is our personal responsibility to align our theology with Theology, as best we can, even though it will still be imperfect. The goal is not perfection; it is alignment with Spirit.

NERD NOOK:
SPIRITUAL BEINGS

Most faith traditions acknowledge the existence of beings we cannot see with our physical sight. Ghosts, angels, demons, jinn, gods, shedim, spirit guides—all different ways religions refer to beings that exist in the spiritual and energetic realm. History and tradition acknowledge the existence of beings we cannot see with our physical eyes in lore, tradition, scripture, medical instructions, and many other historical writings. While many Western countries prioritize rational intellect over intuitive wisdom, spirituality still thrives in the day-to-day life of many families, societies, and cultures.

Why?

Although our understanding and knowledge of our world have expanded through scientific exploration, we still encounter unexplainable phenomena regularly. From ghostly apparitions to angelic interventions, every corner of civilization has a way of making room for beings and experiences beyond our understanding. These phenomena are so prevalent that some researchers are beginning to use science to explore psychic phenomena and human consciousness. The University of Virginia, School of Medicine, is one such organization that has a division of study dedicated to Perceptual Studies where research is conducted on past-lives experiences, near-death experiences, and the neuroscience of psi abilities. These fields of study, coupled with our initial exploration into the world of quantum science, suggest that there is something substantial in our spiritual and psychic experiences that cannot be ignored.

As we watch science intersect with spirituality, we would be foolish to write off our spiritual encounters with energetic entities as purely fiction. Just because we can't explain it yet doesn't mean it isn't real. For now, we can recognize that because every human being is equipped to take in information from both overlaying worlds of the physical and energetic, every human being is also capable of connecting with what we call spiritual beings, and until science catches up with our human experiences of spiritual beings, religious texts are our best guide.

Spiritual beings are typically named and recognized for the quality of their impact on humanity. Lower energies or evil spirits are those who mislead, destroy, and create chaos and mischief. Common names for these energies include demons, devils, and jinn. Higher energies or benevolent beings are those that aid and protect humanity as they seek a good life that benefits themselves, others, and the world. They are known as angels, spirit guides, or ancestors. Faith traditions acknowledge many types of spiritual beings and stress the importance of human discernment when engaging with these entities.

Connection with the Source of All Creation

Consider this for a moment. You are always connected with the power, energy, wisdom, and purpose of your Creator. You are made of the same stuff as all the universe, and you are connected with all the systems and forces within the universe. You are infused with the mysterious force of life and consciousness. You are finite and eternal, according to physics, and you are an integral part of a magnificent whole world, universe, and creation.

The eternal aspect of you is always connected to your source, by whatever name you choose to use: Universe, Great Spirit, Messiah, Allah, HaShem, Akal Purakh, Brahma, or however you have come to know the One who is God of Gods and Chief Diety. This Creator is always available to you. You have access to the One who authored and directed the writing of your sacred texts. You are known by the One who commissioned your life here on earth. You are connected to the Creator of all creation.

I remember being in awe when I first became aware of this reality. I was studying a passage in the Christian Bible and a question arose in my mind. While I was thinking about whom I could ask to gain clarity, I "heard" (clairaudience) in my mind, "Why don't you ask the author?"

I was momentarily stunned by this response and thought to myself, "How would this be possible? The author has died over a thousand years ago!"

"Why don't you ask the author?" The phrase repeated in my mind.

"What do you mean? What author?" I responded.

"Who wrote this book? Who is the author?" the inner voice continued.

"Moses? John? Paul?" I wondered. My brain scanned through the list of biblical authors.

"They wrote it down, but who is the author?" the inner voice continued.

"You mean Spirit? Ahhhh! I can ask Spirit to help me!" Finally, I understood what that small voice was telling me.

Although it took me a minute to understand what my intuition was teaching me, this revelation that the Source of all is connected with me at all times has changed the way I am in the world. The Source of life, the Author of creation, is available to you and connected with you at all times. And this connection is dynamic; it runs both ways through our intuitive senses that are embedded in our energetic selves.

Let that sink in. You are in a dynamic connection with the Source of all wisdom, energy, and purpose in the universe. You have access to all the wisdom, guidance, understanding, and truth through this dynamic relationship. And who better to partner with you along your Selah Journey than the One who knows you perfectly, and wants what is best for the world, including you? Who better to help guide you in your purpose and actions? Who better to provide knowledge and prompts to help you on your way?

Your best, brightest, strongest, wisest, and most loving travel partner for your Selah Journey is your Spiritual Source. Lean in and get ready to expand!

The
POSSIBILITIES

CHAPTER 10

TRANSFORMATION TIME!

Words that make my husband cringe: Honey, I have a great idea!

I had many wonderful influences in my life who taught me how to think outside the box. When I get an idea, my first thoughts are not all the reasons it might not work out, but instead, my head starts figuring out all the ways we can make this "great idea" happen. So when those words—"Honey, I have a great idea"—cross my lips, my husband is confident that my next words are likely to come out of left field. When I uttered those infamous words to my husband one May afternoon, I gave him major credit for not only listening to my spur-of-the-moment proposition but also for agreeing to it.

Let's back up for a moment. At this point in my life, I was a people-oriented introvert, working within a university calendar. I was also a mother of two school-aged children. The spring semester had just finished, and I had only two days before I needed to head out to a professional conference on the other side of the country. Needless to say, as a working, introverted mother of young kids, I needed some solid alone time. I knew I needed it, and my brain had been working overtime trying to figure out how to make the stars align so this needed personal space would appear out of thin air.

Then it hit me! My great idea! I would just drive from Massachusetts to Idaho in two days by myself and make it to the conference with enough energy to tolerate people for one more week. Then I would take one week to slowly drive myself home on my first solo cross-country retreat of sorts, to recharge my social battery. Driving energizes me, so 2,700 miles (4,345 kilometers) shouldn't be a problem, even though I felt drained from all the end-of-semester activity. Surely this was a fantastic idea. All I had to do was pack in one hour, get the family dinner, and then take off before bedtime.

To my husband's credit, he did not call me crazy (although I'm sure he thought so) and after listening to my plea, he agreed.

The road trip was exactly what I needed. I drove through the American countryside, sometimes in silence, and sometimes with the windows down and the music up. I did the professional development stuff and wrapped up my year with a proper bow. Then I returned to the road for one more week of solitude, solo adventuring, and life lessons along the journey. Returning to my family at the end of my trip, I was more present, more grounded, and better prepared for the rhythm summer would bring.

Little did I know, the trip was a foreshadowing of the first Selah Journey that would come a decade later. How so? Well first, I listened to my heart and my body telling me what it needed. I committed to finding a way to give myself the much-needed space to take care of me by recharging my soul after a busy season of life. I chose to allow myself to be a priority and followed the sound advice of my heart.

Second, I allowed myself a space for Sabbath Resting. I know road-tripping isn't everyone's idea of a restful retreat, but I feel freedom and joy while I watch life unfold as the countryside changes. Taking the scenic route to soak in the incredible vistas and traveling at my own pace reunites me with the wonder of this world we live in and the contentment I find in an unhurried life. My mind, soul, and body found rest along the road.

Third, I would occasionally turn off the music and drive in silent prayer and reflection. Talking and listening to Spirit, I gave myself space for the questions and thoughts that were pushed away in the hustle of life. I allowed emotions to surface and took time to tune into where they were coming from. All these moments allowed the gift of reflection to take root in my road trip rhythm.

Lastly, I experienced and recognized deep gratitude. Gratitude to my husband for affirming my "great idea" and sending me on my retreat with blessings. Gratitude to my Creator for the beauty that I witnessed in the mountains, plains, valleys, and rivers. Gratitude for the insights I was gaining as I reflected on my experiences. Gratitude for my friends who supported my trip and cheered me on!

All of this happened because of my Selah Tribe. The support of my husband. The verbal companionship of friends I chatted with by phone along the way. The couches and guest rooms shared with me by more friends along my route. The recommendations of locals for great local food when I went off the beaten path.

All the elements of a Selah Journey were there... I just didn't realize it then.

Time to Start Your Selah Journey

Commit to Yourself

Are you ready to begin your Selah Journey? Learning about how Spirit has accompanied me along the path to my own Selah Journey, I am 100% certain the practices and the process of The Selah Journey have value for every single person.

If you are:

- ⊚ Feeling trapped in a life that isn't working for you, and you don't know how to find a new way through;
- ⊚ Sick and tired of being sick and tired;
- ⊚ Discouraged because you cannot force yourself to be the person others want you to be;
- ⊚ Surviving the challenges of life, but cling to the dream of thriving one day; and/or
- ⊚ Done with making excuses and are ready to transform into the best version of you imaginable.

You are ready. The Selah Journey is your pathway into a life of purpose, passion, and freedom. It is time to embrace the reality that you are just as important as the person next to you, no matter what they do. You are worthy. You are capable. It is time for you to make a commitment to yourself to begin your Selah Journey.

What does that mean? Traveling your Selah Journey involves committing to the five pillars of Selah.

1. **I Choose Me**: Your self-care is your responsibility. As a human being, you have the same inherent worth, value, and potential as every other human on this planet. You are absolutely a worthy investment. The Selah Journey reminds you to embrace your inherent worth and to commit to practices that allow you to walk the path of transformation into the best and highest version of yourself you can be in this life. #IChooseMe

2. **Sabbath Resting**: Life is a balance of rest and work, activity, and stillness. Just like the rhythm of the day, we are tied to a constant cycle of activity while the sun shines and rest when the sun sets. However, we easily get knocked out of balance when we believe our worth is attached to our work and we neglect practices of breathing, sleeping, stillness, and restoration. Sabbath Resting is committing to developing your rhythms of holistic rest that allow you to move toward your best self. #SabbathResting

3. **The Gift of Reflection**: Many of our actions and thoughts are anchored in habits and past experiences. The gift of reflection provides the tools for us to be curious about where our responses and beliefs grew from and allows us to reintegrate them into our lives in a more aligned and true way. Building your reflection practice is a vital step as you take ownership of who you are growing into. #TheGiftOfReflection

4. **Gratitude and Praise**: If we desire a life of joy, freedom, and flow then we need to attune ourselves to seeing how

these positive qualities are already present in our lives. We find what we look for; as our attention is drawn towards what is good and yummy in our lives, we connect with how abundant we already are. Commit to practicing gratitude and giving praise to others and Spirit for the good they bring into your life. It rewires our brains for joy and allows the abundance of goodness to be seen everywhere we look! #GratitudeAndPraise

5. **The Selah Tribe**: Every journey is made better by the people who support us as we travel. Friends, family, acquaintances, and those we have yet to meet all have something to offer us along the way. Be mindful of who you allow into your Selah Tribe. These are your people who will witness, reflect, speak truth in love, comfort, and challenge you all along your transformative journey. #MySelahTribe

I believe you are ready to begin your Selah Journey. And you have everything you need to start. The first step is to make the commitment to yourself that it is time to embrace the possibilities that are in your future and begin walking the Selah path towards more freedom in your life.

Customize the Journey

One of my favorite things about walking my own Selah Journey and witnessing others travel theirs is how incredibly different each path is. The diversity of humanity is a beautiful wonder! Because of that, every single Selah Journey is unique—a fantastic, personalized, one-of-a-kind experience.

The Selah Journey provides the practices that allow you to explore who you are, what has led you to this point in your life, and the direction you are choosing to grow into. It is a journey in which each of us is challenged to shed our attachment to being a victim of our circumstances.

It empowers you to embrace the responsibility and freedom of thriving as exactly who you are! Imagine that! Your dreams, desires, and passions come together to gift you with your purpose and direction in life. You, being the best, brilliant version of yourself, every day. Trading self-judgment for curiosity and exchanging self-doubt for confidence. Because you are brilliantly unique, your journey will be customized and tailored to you. Not your family. Not your friends. Not your enemies. Not your followers. Your Selah Journey is you becoming the youiest you you can be.

Including a life coach, a counselor, or a mentor in your Selah Tribe is another fantastic way you can claim this commitment to yourself. Of course, I would say this! But remember, this isn't about me, it is about you. How do you show yourself you are committed to your own growth and transformation? You put some money where your mouth is. You put a little skin in the game. Studies have shown that we are more likely to follow through on transformative practices like exercise or performance goals when we take steps that cost us something like buying a gym membership or hiring a personal trainer.

The same is true of your personal transformation. Life coaches are experts in change and transformation. Their professional and ethical role is to hold and protect space for you, in confidence, so you can walk your path of transformation. Your life coach is your accountability partner to help you stay the course; your mirror so you can see yourself more clearly; your bullshit alarm when you get squirrelly; your trail guide to supply tools and strategies for the tricky parts; and your best cheerleader because they can see the you that you are becoming. And they celebrate every step with you. Intuitive life coaches will connect you with your inner wisdom so that you can lean on your highest self, your Spiritual Source, and your most trusted guides. If you aren't ready for this type of experience yet, trusted friends are also a fantastic source of support and accountability as well. Find a way to take action on your commitment to walk your Selah Journey by finding a trusted travel partner for accountability, support, and companionship along the way.

Celebrate Your Progress

Did you know that for ten years of my life, I didn't believe I was worth celebrating? This was one of the many untruths I believed during my history with depression. I would hide my birthdate from others, deflect compliments, and recite all the reasons why I was unworthy in order to keep myself "humble." I thank my Creator that this chapter of untruth is behind me because I was miserable. The truth is I am a unique and amazing gift to my family, my community, and this world. You are too! No one else can be you! We need you to be you! You have a story to share, and you deserve to shine! No matter your past, it does not define your future.

The Selah Journey is traveled one step at a time. One decision. One exploration. One moment. One commitment. One step, repeated by another one step, and another one step, and another. When we are on the pathway, sometimes we forget how far we've actually traveled and can easily miss the milestones because we are enveloped in the world of transformation. Celebration is an invaluable practice along your Selah Journey.

Just like our birthdays and anniversaries present us with an annual opportunity to look back on the year past and look ahead to the year that is coming, celebrating our milestones within our Selah Tribe gives us perspective and appreciation for the hard work we do that leads to our freedom. The power of celebration is energizing. When we witness the steps and the commitment we have taken to pursue authentic and aligned freedom, we ignite our gratitude for the journey and our hope for the future. Now, instead of deflecting, I celebrate! I celebrate the month I discovered my Selah Journey. That moment in my history pivoted me out of despair into hope in such a way I cannot turn back. I celebrate the anniversary of my first published chapter, where I took a step of bravery and shared my Selah Journey with the world for the first time. I celebrate the first UAE dirhams I earned from my first paying coaching client. And I have many more celebrations that I am looking forward to in my future.

Your Selah Tribe will provide many benefits for you, like perspective, counsel, and accountability. But most importantly, your tribe is your witness to your commitment, courage, and hard work as you transform into the best and youiest you. As you acknowledge and share your milestones and revelations, your tribe gets to witness your miraculous transformation. A most worthy celebration! Imagine a community that uses celebration to honor one another and create an upward flow of inspiration to fuel each one of us along our path. Stunning.

You have everything you need to begin your Selah Journey. And if you'd like more of what this book has provided, we have a community waiting for you in our exclusive and global Selah Journey space online. It is our virtual hub for all things related to Selah Journey. It is our tribe of people who are all in pursuit of a common goal—living a life of freedom and authenticity where we honor every part of the transformative journey. Just like the individuals who explore these spaces, the community space grows as we grow. And you are invited to join us.

*You have
everything
you need to
begin your
Selah Journey.*

ONE LAST THING

I See Your Courage

I wish you could see what is in my heart as I write these words. I am sitting in a coffee shop, and I can see you sitting across from me. As you have been learning about The Selah Journey, I can feel the hope rising up within you. But every now and again, there is a shadow of doubt that traverses your face. Is it a hesitation that you cannot believe you are worthy of all The Selah Journey holds out for you? Is it a fear of rejection that if others see you truly, they won't like what is there? Is it a voice of untrue belief that you are not capable of such transformation?

I'm not sure what shadow may be attempting to hold you back, but I remember all of the above hesitations and more when I was at rock bottom, spiraling into my deepest fears. If you understand what I am saying, then please hear me loud and clear… I see you. I see the courage you leaned into to read this book. I see the courage it takes you to perhaps believe you are more worthy than you ever imagined. I see the courage you are exerting to push through your fear to see if any hope for you is within reach.

I see your courage. And I honor your courage. And I celebrate your courage.

*What
does love
invite you to
do next?*

When in Doubt, Choose Love

As you consider your next steps, let me ask one final question. What does love invite you to do next? Your Creator loves you beyond your comprehension. What does your Creator invite you to do next? Your highest self loves you perfectly and cannot wait to see you thrive! What does he or she invite you to do next? Those in your family who love you and champion you, what would they invite you to do next? When you consider all your sources of love that support you in this life, what is the next step they are asking you to take?

Take that step. Love calls us into freedom, expansion, growth, and joy. Choose love. Take your next step.

You Are Invited to Your Selah Journey

 You're Invited!

Please RSVP at your earliest convenience. We look forward to having you as part of our tribe.

CELEBRATING IN GRATITUDE

Creating this book has been an incredible journey for me. Just as my first Selah Journey supported me with an incredible tribe of people, so has this journey of publishing my first book. While I filled the role of author for this adventure, a multitalented community of storytellers, teachers, mentors, designers, editors, encouragers, and more participated in providing me with what I needed at just the right moments. My story has become a tool and guide for others thanks to the investments of this beautiful team.

First, I am deeply grateful for my family.

To Stefan, my husband, who gave me the freedom to fall apart so that I could find my way to becoming whole again, who faithfully loved me through the valleys and the mountain tops, and who is the best partner I could have in my life, I love you and could not do this without you.

To my kiddos, Darienne and Micah, who have taught me about the depth of love that came into being the moment you each were born, and who continue to inspire me with their unique personalities and tenacity to persevere. You two are the twin joys of my heart. My mihija and my buddy.

To my parents, Bud and Mimi Smith, who always gave me the best of who they are and showed me who I could become through their stories, their examples, and their presence. You done good. Love you.

And to my siblings—Sarah, you showed me I was worthy of being celebrated before I could admit that for myself. And Caleb, you bring me joy always and have become this helper's best partner. I love you both completely. Thank you for all the ways you have supported my becoming and all of my pursuits.

Next, to my publishing team, who brought my words greater life than I ever could on my own.

To Lanette Pottle, your leadership and expertise in publishing showed me how to put my voice onto ink and paper so that my stories can fly. Your support has made this girl's lifelong dream of writing a book a reality. I cannot thank you enough.

To my technical and creative superstars: To my editor, Domanie Spencer, your watchful and talented eye not only made me a better writer, it encouraged my heart. To my design creator, George B. Stevens, your designs uniquely conveyed my story perfectly. I can't wait to work with you both again.

To my photographer (and dive buddy), Charlotte Van Rooyen, you provided me with a photo shoot that allowed me to feel beautiful and vibrant, and captured the joy I feel when I am working with my clients. Thank you for the laughter and friendship you always bring to our adventures together.

To my advanced readers: Amy Loyall, Lara Barrett, Kelly Bowley, and Shawna Kuyntz, thank you for being the first people to share your honest and loving feedback with my first vulnerable draft. Your words have made this a better story for all to enjoy.

To my treasured mentors and guides: Heather Alice Shea, April Adams Pertuis, and Alexandra Taketa, you three invited me into your respective worlds amid my messy metamorphosis. You collectively showed me my worth, my talent, and my abilities. You lavished love and wisdom on me and set me on this brilliant path of The Selah Journey. You were divinely appointed angels along my path, and a forever part of my story, now and in the days yet to come.

To my very first Selah Tribe: Jen White, Jill Rice, Casey Taylor, Shelley Hart, Brooks Taylor, Mauny Rothler, Kim Beam, and Lisa Spencer. When you met me in my meltdown, we had no idea which way I would go! (And it was dicey there for a while!) But I would not have made it through without you. Your gifts of shelter, meals, counsel, presence, and wisdom provided what I needed at the perfect moments. I dearly love each one of you.

To my Flip Flop girls: Robin Hackney, Amy Loyall, Shawna Kuyntz, and Erin Lubowicz—y'all are just the best cheerleaders in the world! Your confidence and encouragement made the journey from idea to book a joy to travel. Thank you for everything! Especially the hugs, laughter, and love.

To Nader Otaibi, my Habibi, who opened me up to my newest obsession, diving in the beauty of the underwater world, and reminded me that our differences make us richer when we share our passions with each other.

To my clients and readers, who have trusted me with their stories and have allowed me to witness the magnificence of their own Selah Journeys. Your courage inspires me daily.

And finally, to my God, the Great Spirit, Creator, Source of all Truth, my Light, and my Life—who orchestrated sacred appointments with exactly the right people at exactly the right moments, who whispered *Selah* when I needed it most, and who has been the most faithful travel companion for my journey here on earth. To you I give all the glory. Amen.

The Selah Journey was never meant to be traveled alone. I hold so much love, admiration, and joy for each of you who have walked alongside me in this journey. This book is our shared creation. I could not have asked for a better tribe.

In Deepest Gratitude,

Cami

RESOURCES AND SOURCES

Chapter 2: You Are Here

Van der Kolk, Bessel A. *The Body Keeps the Score: Brain, Mind, and Body in the Healing of Trauma*. New York: Viking, 2014.

A groundbreaking examination of how trauma affects the brain and body, offering innovative treatments for reclaiming lives.

Mayo Clinic. "Stress Management." Mayo Clinic. Last modified March 4, 2024. https://www.mayoclinic.org/healthy-lifestyle/stress-management/in-depth/stress/art-20046037.

Comprehensive resource explaining the long-term effects of stress on physical and mental health.

World Health Organization. "Stress: Questions and Answers." WHO. Accessed March 4, 2024. https://www.who.int/news-room/questions-and-answers/item/stress.

Authoritative information on stress as a global health concern, including definitions and impacts.

Chapter 3: Destination: You

Hollinger, Dennis P. *Head, Heart & Hands: Bringing Together Christian Thought, Passion and Action*. Downers Grove: InterVarsity Press, 2005.

Explores the integration of intellect, emotions, and actions in creating a holistic approach to personal development and faith.

HeartMath Institute. "Science of the Heart." HeartMath Institute. Accessed March 4, 2024. https://www.heartmath.org/research/science-of-the-heart/

Research on heart-brain connections and the heart's electromagnetic field, offering insights into coherence and emotional self-regulation.

Chapter 4: Sabbath Resting

Walker, Matthew. *Why We Sleep: The New Science of Sleep and Dreams*. New York: Scribner, 2017.

Illuminating research on sleep's critical role in physical health, emotional well-being, cognitive function, and overall quality of life.

Heschel, Abraham Joshua. *The Sabbath: Its Meaning for Modern Man*. New York: Farrar, Straus and Giroux, 2005.

A poetic exploration of Sabbath as a sanctuary in time and its relevance for contemporary living.

Awan, Naeem M. et al. "Sleep in Islamic Culture and the Quran." *Sleep and Vigilance* 5 (2021): 33-40. https://www.ncbi. nlm.nih.gov/pmc/articles/PMC3183634/.

Scholarly examination of sleep practices and concepts in Islamic tradition, comparing ancient wisdom with modern sleep science.

Chapter 6: Gratitude and Praise

Chowdhury, Madhuleena Roy. "The Neuroscience of Gratitude and Effects on the Brain." PositivePsychology.com. April 9, 2019. https://positivepsychology.com/neuroscience-of-gratitude/.

Research-based article detailing how gratitude practices physically alter brain function and improve mental health.

Steindl-Rast, Brother David. "Gratefulness." A Network for Grateful Living. Accessed March 4, 2024. https://grateful.org.

Resources from the "grandfather of gratitude" on cultivating thankfulness as a pathway to joy.

Chapter 9: Your Spiritual Source

University of Virginia School of Medicine. "Division of Perceptual Studies." UVA. Accessed March 4, 2024. https://med. virginia.edu/perceptual-studies/.

Academic research on consciousness, near-death experiences, and other phenomena related to spirituality and intuition.

JOIN THE SELAH JOURNEY COMMUNITY

Find Your Tribe. Share Your Journey. Transform Together.

Have you ever wished for a space where others truly understand your journey toward self-discovery? A place where you can be authentic, vulnerable, and celebrated for who you truly are?

The Selah Journey isn't meant to be traveled alone.

Our global community of fellow travelers provides:

- Support when the path feels challenging
- Encouragement from those who have walked similar roads
- Celebration of your milestones and breakthroughs
- Resources to support your journey
- Early access to upcoming events and workshops
- And so much more

Scan the QR code below to join us today:

Your journey matters. Your story matters. And we can't wait to welcome you home.

LET'S CONNECT

Begin Your Personal Selah Journey

Are you ready to move from reading about The Selah Journey to experiencing its transformative power for your own life? We are here to help!

Personal Coaching & Mentorship

Take the first step towards reclaiming your authentic self with personalized support tailored to your unique journey. Discover what is possible when you have an experienced guide by your side.

Speaking & Workshops

Transform your team, event, or community with the principles of The Selah Journey. We create engaging and interactive sessions to inspire a selah lifestyle and authentic alignment.

Scan the QR code for a FREE 30-minute discovery call:

Find Us Online

Facebook
www.facebook.com/theselahjourney/

Instagram
www.instagram.com/theselahjourney/

LinkedIn
www.linkedin.com/in/camirfoerster/

Website
www.theselahjourney.com

Your transformation begins with a single step. Let's take it together.

A LITTLE MORE
ABOUT THE AUTHOR

Cami Foerster knows what it means to lose yourself while taking care of everyone else. As the founder of The Selah Journey and an intuitive life coach, her path to helping others find their authentic selves began with her own crisis—when panic attacks and exhaustion forced her to flee her life and rediscover who she truly was.

Growing up in northern California before experiencing the United States coast to coast, Cami now divides her time between Colorado's majestic Rocky Mountains and the wild desert of the United Arab Emirates. For decades, she was a helper, mentor, and guide to others while neglecting her own well-being. Her compulsion to care for everyone eventually led to a breaking point that became her breakthrough—a personal Selah Journey that transformed her understanding of self-worth, rest, and authentic living.

Drawing on the ancient concept of *Selah*—a practice of pausing for rest, honest reflection, and gratitude—Cami developed a framework that rescued her from burnout and depression. Now, she shares these life-changing practices with others who find themselves weary, lost, or disconnected from their true purpose.

A bestselling author and educator who describes herself as "the dancing mermaid," Cami combines intuitive wisdom with practical tools, helping clients reconnect with their highest selves. She is building a global community for those embarking on their own Selah Journeys, with the goal of creating a worldwide movement empowering people to become their best selves.

When not writing, speaking, or mentoring, you'll find Cami savoring life's simple pleasures: the perfect cup of black coffee, nature's wonders, or meaningful conversations with friends over whiskey.

PAY IT FORWARD

Help us expand our reach! Personal and honest reviews are invaluable to us for spreading the good word and connecting with others who are looking for our message. The Selah Journey is committed to building a supportive and authentic community, and you can help us achieve this by sharing your reading experience with others.

Let us know what inspired you, challenged you, equipped you, and encouraged you. Share your thoughts and contribute to the ongoing conversation.

We want to hear from you!

Made in the USA
Monee, IL
14 June 2025

19295568R00118